D0642926

Teacher at Point Blank

Confronting Sexuality, Violence, and Secrets in a Suburban School

JO SCOTT-COE

aunt lute books

san francisco

Aunt Lute Books
P.O. Box 410687
San Francisco, CA 94141
www.auntlute.com

Cover design: Amy Woloszyn, amymade.com
Text design: Amy Woloszyn

Senior Editor: Joan Pinkvoss
Managing Editor: Shay Brawn
Production: Soma Baral, Ashley Bonifacio, Noelle de la Paz, Chenxing Han, Vanessa Nava, and Kara Owens

Excerpt from "This Gun Is Real" (*Mansions*, 1990) by Donna Hilbert used by permission of the author.

Funding for the production of *Teacher at Point Blank* was provided in part by support from the Vessel Foundation and Three Dog Foundation.

Library of Congress Cataloging-in-Publication Data

Printed in the U.S.A. on acid-free paper

10 9 8 7 6 5 4 3 2 1

I do not permit a woman to act as teacher, or in any way to have authority over a man; she must be quiet…She will be saved through childbearing, provided she continues in faith and love and holiness — her chastity, of course, being taken for granted.

—1 Timothy 2: 12, 15

Our writing students give us an easy out for our maternal urge to live vicariously, to measure and define our creativity in terms of our enabling others to be creative. Our silence feeds on the speech of these important, often beloved others…
[T]heir inscription is enabled by our erasure.

—Diana Hume George, "Mothering in the Academy"

…[I]f we still had ambitions, ideas about ourselves as people in our own right — well, we were simply freaks, neurotics, and we confessed our sin to priest or psychoanalyst, and tried hard to adjust.

—Betty Friedan, *The Feminine Mystique*

Table of Contents

Introduction

And I go in dread of sentimentality.
—Virginia Wolf, *A Writer's Diary*

Shortly before I left my teaching job to begin work on this project, one male colleague, overhearing me comment about the collusion of textbook companies and testing corporations, rolled his eyes and sighed. "For God's sake," he interrupted, "just have a child."

Little could he know that this book—or my idea of it—had already arrived as a kind of unplanned, uneasy, and not altogether welcome pregnancy. Its inception began more than ten years ago with a phone call in the summer of 2000, during my honeymoon. My husband, Justin, and I had driven across the deserts of Southern California and Arizona to the mountains of New Mexico, where we were spending a week in a Ruisdoso timeshare. Shortly after our arrival, Justin received a voice message from the college where he had just completed a semester as a part-time adjunct English instructor. The dean's message was urgent. My husband must call back immediately. A student and his father were unhappy with a D+ grade.

I braced myself as Justin punched in the phone number. At the time, I'd been teaching high school English for eight years in a suburban setting, so I was used to the ambush of sudden, off-season accountability. Although this wasn't *my* student or *my* dean, I felt a familiar grip of anxiety rise into my shoulders. Throughout the spring semester before our wedding, I had already learned of difficulties Justin experienced in this case, and I heard him now recount them aloud, as if offering legal testimony: Yes, the student had missed multiple sessions of a college writing class that met only once a week. The student had skipped an entire essay assignment altogether (despite encouragement to turn it in late, even for full credit), and his final research paper had been a disaster. The student attributed all absences and missing work to his rigorous schedule as an Olympics-bound athlete with competitions and practices to attend. No, Justin didn't bring his attendance or grade books along to the cabin, but he certainly *had* maintained records. Yes, he had also kept copies of all grading criteria along with the student's work in a file, at home. Yes, he would be happy to share these when we returned. No, it was no trouble at all.

As I sensed those fingers of intrusion curl around us — too easily — from nearly one thousand miles away, my husband's last statement, a sadly familiar lie ("No trouble at all") seemed to marry us in a new way. Justin may have witnessed such phone conversations as I made them (or listened as I attempted to summarize them afterwards), but this was a first for him. Weren't college instructors beyond such demands?

Unfortunately, "hiding the trouble" seemed to be an increasingly unhealthy and unspoken part of our work with students. (While it may have long been routine for colleagues at the primary and secondary levels, it was steadily creeping into the experiences of faculty at colleges and universities, too.) I witnessed how accounts of what happened in our classrooms could be demanded and then abruptly dismissed, regardless of the trouble: student grades, attendance, cheating/plagiarism, disruptive or even threatening behavior. Hyper-vigilance and self-doubt about all aspects of teaching could morph into disturbing habits of denial, self-effacement, even complicity.

Of course, Justin handled his situation professionally, despite the tension, and we managed to enjoy the rest of our brief time away. Yet hanging over us that rainy week was the knowledge that, upon our return, the dean would review Justin's documentation and would decide whether to support the grade or to invalidate it. Like other instructors in similar situations, Justin was simply a defendant in a "court" that pitted teachers against students. We could not be trusted to be fair or conscientious. And we could be easy targets of blame for failure, lack of judgment, or incompetence—whether or not it was ours to own. Even though the dean, in the end, did support Justin's assessment, the two of us had also been vividly reminded that, as teachers, our personal lives had no serious or sacred boundaries. We ought to be thinking about students and grades at every moment. Even after the semester had ended, even on a honeymoon, we were under the gun.

Something else happened that week. In one of our many forays into used bookstores, I found a copy of Betty Friedan's *The Feminine Mystique*, a soft blue paperback with heavy-grained, yellowing pages darkened at the edges but otherwise immaculate—perhaps never read. I started reading the text in an aisle of the shop and found the book difficult to put down, feeling drawn as if by some pull of gravity to Friedan's description of "the problem that has no name" among women whose lives were centered exclusively (working class voices might say, *rather luxuriously*) upon raising their children. This visceral attraction was ironic, for two reasons. In the conservative, military household of my childhood, where my parents made financial sacrifices to assure that my sister and I could attend good parochial schools, the political writers of choice had been William F. Buckley and Phyllis Schlafly—not "libs" like Friedan or her contemporary, Gloria Steinem. While I had long since discovered and relished texts by feminists as diverse as Mary Wollstonecraft, Simone De Beauvoir, Susan Griffin, Tillie Olsen, bell hooks, Nancy Chodorow, Julia Kristeva, Deborah Tannen, and Gloria Anzaldúa, I had never read Friedan. *The Feminine Mystique* represented a point of view that my parents had rejected the way they rejected N.O.W., *Roe v. Wade*, the Equal Rights Amendment, and school busing.

The second irony strikes me now as more relevant, and it provided a starting point from which I began to read, study, and question on my own: Except for my whiteness, I actually had little in common with the subjects of Friedan's study. Although, like them, I was married, I had entered that state at a later period of my life (at 31 years old), and I had married a man slightly younger than myself. We had blended our last names together. I was (so-far) childless. Furthermore, I worked as a professional and fully certificated teacher who had earned a graduate degree in her subject matter. I was actively writing and publishing (though not to the extent I desired, largely due to the weight of my student caseloads). For the moment, I was also the primary breadwinner of our small household. Still, aspects of my experience as a teacher seemed related to the dilemmas of a generation of women who had proven themselves intellectually in college, yet felt blindsided by the unanticipated costs of trading in their own interests and careers for motherhood and homemaking.

During the next few years, I sought to examine this association more deeply. There were obvious elements — and Justin and I discussed them often: the work with children or adolescents in relative isolation; the demoralizing combination of scrutiny and lack of support; the ways teacher credibility — even safety — depended upon backup from other people who rarely if ever visited classrooms, whether parents, administrators (often male), or campus aides — all figures to whom teachers had to make special and sometimes hands-tying appeals for help.

I was indeed earning a paycheck — a good one — yet the disjunction between the fantasies or "mystiques" of teaching and the realities of the daily job seemed to parallel ideologies of middle class femininity and motherhood critiqued by Friedan and many other writers. Strangely, the relative financial security of tenure and the glossy, superficial pretense of intellectual, "instructional" work made the disjunctions more disturbing. Because teachers' daily labor took place outside the view of other adults, it invited sentimentality on one hand and harsh judgments ("that's not real work") on the other. Our achievements were vicarious, often measured by degrees of sacrifice to the idol of childhood.

I also began to notice how the schizophrenia of reverence and contempt for women, especially mothers, was mirrored for teachers in popular culture and public policy. It didn't help that I worked at a nice school with a green lawn "where bad things didn't happen," and where parents with money and privilege tended to regard teacher work as glorified day care. Silences loomed.

And no wonder. Every day, for nine months out of every year, I worked in a classroom with other people's kids. In positive fantasies, I was supposed to be the all-sacrificing school ma'am (schoolmarm) or *alma mater* — literally, foster mother — or (in a reprise of a Victorian theme first savaged by Virginia Woolf, more recently critiqued by Berenice Malka Fisher) an "angel in the classroom," nurturing little darlings, or saving starving souls. In negative images, I was cast as an inferior surrogate, a parental rival, a babysitter, an overpaid public servant, or an incompetent paper pusher gouging the system, lazily secreting my government paychecks while hiding behind a classroom of kiddies (a stereotype that evokes a powerfully racist-classist disparagement of "the welfare mother"). These images can become so pervasive and so powerful that teachers themselves, grateful for earning tenure yet simultaneously acculturated in habits of institutional obedience, learn that they have a vested interest in perpetuating the fantasy.

None of these images acknowledged the complex humanity of teachers. None offered much room for our own distinct intellects or gifts. The assumption seemed to be that we didn't — or shouldn't — have any. (No doubt this was an attitude tied to an overall decline in aptitudes and ambition of teacher candidates since 1964, when long-sought Civil Rights legislation created wider and more lucrative career options for motivated women with college degrees.) There was certainly no room for frailty or imperfections, either. Common depictions also suggested an either/or dichotomy between the selfishness of "my needs" and primacy of "kids' needs," a zero-sum equation all too familiar for mothers. Our authority tended to be diminished or erased, or else it was characterized negatively as cruel authoritarianism — somehow lumped in with a long-vanished, switch-wielding frontier schoolmaster or the tyrannically cartoonish Pink Floyd monster. A vague notion of "caring" or "niceness" became the ultimate virtue, supplanting knowledge, courage, or fairness.

The result sometimes was a bizarre co-dependent relationship with students as teachers struggled to please everyone, to accommodate disgraceful gaps in the system (say, spending large amounts of personal funds on student materials), or to fulfill other people's ideal expectations — at times to an unhealthy degree. Like myself, many of the teachers I knew and worked with — conscientious, dedicated, smart people — could be swallowed by work, with little room in their lives for much else. Teachers I knew who had young kids of their own, or were primary caregivers outside of school, seemed caught in a continuous tug-of-war between the service they were expected to deliver at school — with caseloads ranging from 160 to 200 adolescents every day — and the human beings they sought to be at home. Because there was limited permission (often self-imposed) to talk freely about what teaching was really like, we could find ourselves at equal turns angry, depressed and self-medicating, knee-jerk defiant, or willfully over-cheerful. If a conversation turned towards the darker aspects of our real-time work, a colleague saying we were "getting too negative" would shut us down. Most of my colleagues — in English departments specifically, and in the K-12 compulsory system generally — were women.

After Justin and I returned from our honeymoon, I spent three more years teaching in the same setting, unable to stop contemplating how deeply my experiences of class and gender seemed to intersect with the professional life to which I thought I had committed. My changing awareness did not make the job easier. I had several increasingly strange and devastating student incidents that were very hard to recover from. I was elected chair of our large department, not knowing that I'd leave the school and change my professional path at the end of a single two-year term.

To make sense of things, to put my experiences as a teacher and my memories as a student into a broader perspective, I started to devour whatever reading I could find. Some progressive researchers (such as John Holt, Alfie Kohn, John Taylor Gatto, Bill Ayers) had been arguing for years that a "one size fits all" approach was bad for students as individuals, but the translation of these ideas seemed to be that ideal teachers teach well in exactly the same way—and needed to be told by a Doctor Spock of Teaching what to do. Still other researchers, such as Jonathan Kozol, bore compelling and necessary witness to the generational poverty and unjust, decrepit learning conditions of students in urban centers, yet somehow merely lumped teachers into an inhuman and unsympathetic part of the school machinery. The teacher memoirs I found seemed only to repeat, however beautifully, the same truisms: While teaching was tough, everything was worthwhile, for the sake of the children.

Of all of my independent study during those years, I was most grateful to find some research witnessing the impact of gender and sexuality on faculty, yet the most powerful resources came from outside the U.S.—from Canada, Australia, and the United Kingdom. Paulo Freire is still the most prominent thinker I've located who has explicitly acknowledged and critiqued the notion of teaching as a "fall back" career for women prior to marriage. I did find university scholars in fields of education, English, and creative writing who sharply addressed the feminization and decreased status of the professoriate, yet none of them acknowledged the premises of neglect and contempt that had been systematically established among teachers in K-12 for almost one hundred years. I also found myself gravitating towards the work of a few American researchers, such as Susan Ohanian and Stephen Krashen, who discussed the connection between *student* learning styles and *teacher* learning/ instructional styles as a feature of healthy, productive schools.

At the end of this decade, feminization is increasingly on the radar of the academy—both as research question, and as blind-spot. The MLA's *Profession 2009* reported an overall decline in tenured faculty at four-year research universities, as well as an increase in part time (low-status, low-security) appointments, with women still holding the vast majority of such positions. Yet while the Autumn 2009 cover of *American Scholar* depicted a female English teacher standing in front of an empty classroom, the male writer's lament about the "decline" in English departments never once acknowledged (admitted?) the gender shift in English, or in the humanities generally. Ironically, Martin Mills, an Australian scholar, called attention *ten years earlier* to the "pink collar" aspects of school work as a gendering process — and also asked readers to consider how the arts and humanities have been feminized (or "queered") while technology, business, and sciences have come to suggest masculinity. Certainly this code is established long before students enter colleges or universities.

As part of my research, I have accumulated a messy archive of articles and advertisements, paying close attention to language that describes teachers and their jobs in popular culture. What I have found are important gaps that connect the social roles of women and teachers. For example, Caitlin Flanagan's exposé on the "nanny wars" in the March 2004 *Atlantic* suggested that many "liberated" and upper class working women were exploiting cheap domestic labor to help raise their children — until they went to school. In 2005, *Time* and *Newsweek* ran dueling cover stories the exact same week in February: the former featuring "What Teachers Hate About Parents" and the latter addressing "The Myth of the Perfect Mother" (both covers featuring a woman at the center).

From this subconscious mythology of teacher domestication comes an unsettling and overt permission for gendered, latently violent disrespect and disregard. Not long ago, Hardee's/Carl's Jr. ran a back-to-school TV burger campaign depicting a white teacher performing pelvic thrusts on her desk while white rapper "boyz" flashed brass knuckles and sang about "flat buns." A woman teacher who sued Los Angeles Unified School District for not intervening when she was sexually harassed by a group of privileged, suburban students saw a jury verdict in her favor overruled by a judge, who asserted that teachers trade their civil rights to a safe workplace for the privilege of educating children. (The judge was himself married to a longtime teacher.)

Exploitative assumptions and degrading fantasies about teachers' work dehumanize school settings, making them all-too-easy targets for violence on a larger, more institutional scale. We may not need to be reminded that in the decade following the tragedy at Columbine, we saw a succession of student rampage shootings, with the most deadly assault occurring on a university campus. But we also must acknowledge the pervasive martial tendencies emerging from national school policy as well. The 9/11 attacks and increased anti-terror surveillance coincided with a drastic increase of standardized testing under the No Child Left Behind Act (NCLB), which not only created a barrage of testing requirements and school ranking systems, but also mandated campuses to provide student data to military recruiters in exchange for federal funding. NCLB also resulted in the explosion of an unregulated, privatized testing industry that now drives education reform, essentially demanding experienced teachers to concede their professional incompetence to captains of the for-profit industrial sector. Obama's Race to the Top legislation has so far extended the NCLB trend, with Secretary of Education Arne Duncan now a leading national advocate for increased privatization (corporate "outsourcing") of public schools as well as expanding the number of public military academies. It is unsurprising that notorious war profiteer Eric Prince of Blackwater (now Xe) announced in a 2009 *Vanity Fair* interview his desire to teach high school history.

The more I studied, the more exhausting and unwieldy the prospect of synthesizing material for this book seemed to be. Something else bothered me, too: popular writing about education felt divided into two dominant camps—simple memoir and highly academic analysis. Memoirs tend to emphasize exceptionality among teachers, schools, and students. Analyses tend to be predictably prescriptive about solutions, checklists, methods, and formulae.

In fact, I didn't find much room in these texts for my experiences or for my voice. Nor did I see much room for the messy, real-life struggles of my colleagues. The more I read and listened, the more I saw the need for books that might challenge brittle categorizations tending to divide (or to evade) a broader audience. In my limited way, I wanted to address a wider and more open world of readers, composed not exclusively of teachers and professors or education policy specialists, but also former students, parents, new teachers or longtime veterans, and anyone who has ever wondered, "Why did this happen? And this? And this?" I was far more interested in examining questions and dilemmas than I was attracted to commercial (often gimmicky) school "solutions" that have historically frustrated teachers and yanked generations of annoyed students from one approach or strategy to another.

For years, researchers have discussed how students recognize and absorb patterns of confinement, compulsion, and silence that can distort and traumatize their experiences in classrooms or school systems. But the effects of such patterns have rarely, if ever, been examined or acknowledged with any depth from the perspectives of people who work as their teachers. Why wouldn't we connect these experiences together, and why have we assumed that adults and young people working in such close proximity day after day would remain unaffected by one another? If we want students to turn to adults for help in schools (and there's research showing that students *don't*), that means we have to face what we see.

Ultimately, this book explores intersections between "creativity" and "research," between "personal" and "political," between "insider" and "outsider" points of view. Sometimes my exploration has felt dangerous because I was treading into material about which I had been trained to remain politely silent. Though always describing real events, patterns, or people, I have condensed or collapsed material and shaded identities. All names of students, faculty, staff, and administrators have been changed or omitted altogether—except in the case of my former teacher and colleague Neil Webb, who died in 2004.

At its heart, this book attempts to capture a type of school violence that occurs long before a kid pulls out a gun—a violence that has emerged from and is perpetuated by expectations of class and gender, suburban ideals of family, and fetishized constructions of both "teacher" and "student." Kids in school already know of this violence, though it may not be easily named, or may be called many different things. Talk to students about pressures to succeed, to choose the "right" schools, to fit into brittle categories framed by gender, ethnicity, and social status. Talk to students who don't quite fit, or who try to live between two worlds.

For now, simply, I am asking that we recognize the complex humanness of teachers—to interrogate patterns of silence and erasure that make it difficult to have healthier, more realistic and thus *more vibrant* teaching relationships with students. It's sad that this feels, on some level, like a great deal to request. In her critique of motherhood as a social institution, Adrienne Rich writes: "[I]t is not enough to let our children go; we need selves of our own to return to." One might add: We need selves of our own to begin with. For what else is graduation, but an annually emptying nest?

At an age when many women were planning their families, I found myself called to a differently fulfilling and challenging path. My choice has been to accept, and eventually to welcome, a full life for this book and any related projects that follow. I understand this as both a privilege and responsibility, not unlike my daily work as a teacher, and I do not claim to speak for or to appease anyone else.

During eighteen years working in classrooms, I have had thousands of kids to whom I have already offered my imperfect best. With this book, however, I seek to recognize—to honor—those many unsung, high-strung, odd, and beautiful colleagues who give their own best selves in plain sight and virtual obscurity. I dedicate this book to them.

Teaching at Point Blank

Their youth is touching, but I know I can't be deceived by it. The young ones are often the most dangerous, the most fanatical, the jumpiest with their guns...You have to go slowly with them.
— Margaret Atwood, *The Handmaid's Tale*

The campus buildings could be cell blocks dried out in the valley heat. Chain-link fencing, cement and brick configurations, piles of construction debris, metal frames, fiberglass and drywall, awnings, unpaved paths, and rows of trailer rooms assemble an empty ghetto. A dead city.

Colors collude in a demoralized palette: cadaver grey, cinder orange, fecal brown, army green, madhouse white. It is difficult to break anything here, more difficult to fix what is broken. There are few windows, no delicate flourishes of style. Nothing says, "be careful" or "this is important." What distantly resembles art is merely cartoonish: Across the side wall of an administration building, the picture of a wildcat sprawls under the school name, under the state seal of distinction, all on yellow background.

Plastic signs are screwed into structures across the site: Needles, pill bottles, guns, and grenades are sketched into circles with lines drawn through them. Above it all, the mantra of zero tolerance: "This is a drug and weapon free campus."

So I taught English for eleven years at my former high school and then pulled myself out, severed a career in half to accept a modest writing fellowship at a local university. The choice cost me in tangible ways: I abandoned the security of tenure, a stable salary with paid medical benefits and a pension plan. I let go of my reputation as a highly regarded instructor in one of the community's best schools, one with a proud tradition of alumni teachers.

Not long after my exit, I ran into a former administrator near the university library. He left the same year I did, moving up the ranks to become principal at his own school. "You always really cared about The Kids," he said, implying the capital letters. He looked past me, at cars entering the parking lot. "I suppose this is just better for you now."

I might as well have left a child in a basket on some random doorstep. I might as well have walked out on my husband or disowned my mother.

After I left, the administration put out a staff survey: *How would you describe the feeling you get as a member of our staff? Do you feel that we as a staff share a feeling of family? What obstacles do you feel exist that prevent us from bonding more closely as a faculty?*

I thought about how the demands of teaching had made me feel too burdened and isolated to have children of my own. How, just recently married and approaching my mid-thirties, I had already donated my most fertile and energetic years to The Kids.

"So...what are you doing?" a former teacher-colleague asked. I guessed I had lost my place at the center of gravity and turned into a figment, some kind of shadow. She pressed again, though I had told her about my research several times before: "Hm? What are you doing now?"

I've forgotten now whatever answer I attempted. Amnesia was everywhere. I wanted to reject it, to remember and re-learn.

In Neil Duncan's 1999 study of sexual bullying among adolescents at schools in England, interviews with male and female students reveal consequences for girls who say "no" to boys demanding a ruler, a piece of paper, last night's homework, a pen. Special names proclaim their reluctance to serve: Bitch, Cow, Slag, Dog.

Some girls keep boys in check with sexual insults: Perv, Fag, Poof.

Males target other males who don't fit the "boy-code" with similar words. They assault peers who seem too gentle, who get along too well with girls.

Duncan reports that male physical attacks on females are rare, but he also cites a "foreboding atmosphere" which keeps potential targets in check.

Male teachers are vulnerable unless they affirm authority through physical horseplay or force — whether actual or threatened. Male teachers' vulnerability increases with age as their perceived virility declines.

Female teachers become acclimated to overt and covert sexual disrespect and suspicion. They do not report acts of harassment to administration and even downplay reports made to them by students.

In one scenario, a student goes into a sex-hate tirade when his female teacher offers a fairly ordinary reproof for misbehavior. Duncan wonders if the student's aggression would be so intense without an audience of male peers.

Duncan cites other research suggesting that patterns of denial in schools contribute to an emotional "hardening" of young men.

Local news: At Chaffey High School in Ontario, California, a boy is caught with a loaded gun in his backpack. Officials cannot decide whether the offense merits expulsion because, as the principal says on camera, "We had no indication that he was going to use it on campus." He also says something about having no experience dealing with "this sort of thing."

The report cuts to material from several weeks earlier, when three Chaffey High School youths admitted to killing an old man in a local park. Footage shows investigators working behind crime scene tape near bushes and trees, shows one person with plastic gloves placing a blanket over a heap on the ground.

As a novice teacher, I had occasionally wished for video footage of incidents in my classroom, believing such documentation would convince parents that I wasn't just another "mean bitch," a

23

hysterical female out to get their child. After a few years working, I learned it was more complicated than that. I watched colleagues — often women — enlist support regarding student behavior, poor attendance, or straggling grades, only to return from parent and administrator meetings feeling accused and guilty, or worse. I saw many raise their tolerance for poor behavior, decide to inflate grades, or plainly resolve never to ask for assistance again.

One colleague, who had just moved to southern California to start a new life after a physically abusive marriage, made a fairly direct analogy: "Blaming myself is all too familiar," she said. One afternoon, a student irritated by the B-minus on his grade report grabbed her into a headlock and yelled, "I'll fuckin' kill you!" While she was disturbed when reporting the incident to the discipline office, the teacher also said she honestly believed the student was "playing around." Yet she was depressed by her administrative interrogation following the report. "I'm always wrong, feeling like I have to apologize," she said. "The men in the office just sat there in a row, across the desk, questioning me."

Events off-campus made me even less certain about the weight of female voice as testimony, no matter what the evidence happened to be. In a notorious 2004 Orange County gang rape case that made national news ("The Haidl Trial"), three young men were accused of sexually assaulting an unconscious sixteen-year-old girl, then penetrating her with a pool cue, juice can, a lighted cigarette. They made a videotape of the alleged attack, showing it off as a trophy afterwards. Another kid took the tape and turned it over to authorities.

The result was a hung jury that couldn't decide whether the girl was unconscious or faking it, even when she urinated on herself, even when her limbs flopped about on the pool table. The prosecution moved to appeal.

Within two weeks of that initial verdict, the central suspect, Gregory Haidl, was arrested for a second rape charge, and then, weeks later, for accumulated violations of bail: drinking, possessing marijuana, trespassing, causing a car accident. Reports gave his age as almost twenty, but his milky skin, blank eyes, cold and resigned hyphen mouth seemed all too familiar — and too young: he could have easily passed for a high school freshman. His brow in mugshots was strained and watchful, framed in that perpetual question: "What? What did I do?"

A male teacher-friend commiserated with me on the phone: "I *know* that face."

Haidl was finally jailed to await the appeals trial. His father, a wealthy and prominent sheriff, was an ultimate figurehead of male authority. Most chilling was his declaration to the *Los Angeles Times* that he would never watch the videotape allegedly made by his own son in his own house.

I imagined being Haidl's teacher in prior years, calling home if I caught him cheating or drunk, falling behind or looking at porn in class. What would his father have said to me? Would I have learned, as I did with other students, that it was no use to bother calling?

Sunday afternoon teacher depression sets in around three p.m. Too many needs to fulfill, impossible to satisfy. I push my gradebook aside, try not to think about lesson plans and student conferences. At least I fend off a migraine.

I switch on cable, find Eyes Wide Shut. *Under guise of cape and mask, the husband — Tom Cruise — sneaks into a sexual club reserved for the ultra-privileged. When he obeys the order to remove his mask, his eyebrows, the bangs across his forehead, look sheepish and kidlike. He's ordered to remove his clothes. Suddenly, the camera cuts and zooms in on a naked woman in stilettos and feathered mask. She looks down from the mezzanine and shouts: "Let him go! I am ready to redeem him!"*

Here the expected sacrifice for the irresponsible male — the good whore narrative — makes me tired. I mute the volume for the last half hour of film, comb through a stack of student essays on my lap: two hundred pages, easy. The light in the room has changed to orange shade and shadow. There's a heaviness to the papers, a visceral loneliness in the paragraphs, the typos, the whiteout marks. There's my own unpaid overtime, the crabbed feeling in my hands and the bend of my neck after hours of concentrating and cramming in comments I hope – but don't know – will help. The smallness I feel in the repetition.

I think of the student who comes back to me each time, no matter what: "You just didn't get it." He points to the middle of his paper. "You can't mark me down for that." His mother calls for meetings, repeating the same.

To drown out the dread, I click the sound back on. The final scene: Tom Cruise and his wife walk through a toy shop. He has told his wife everything. They stop near shelves with stuffed bears and girl-dolls in florid dresses.

Waiting for absolution, he looks at her.

Two boys in front rows conferred across an aisle when I entered to start class. The tardy bell rang. Students were getting their books out – the usual noise. I shuffled through a folder of graded exams to return, pulled out a roll sheet. I liked this class, second period, very much.

"You're tall," one called out. "You like being tall? How tall are you?"

I smiled. I told them I was five foot ten. Other students listened. Some of the girls watched me closely.

"Why you wear heels then?" someone else called out. Another male voice.

I waited, tried to twinkle my expression as I searched to make eye contact around the room. I realized that I was wearing a red miniskirt suit and opaque black tights. The heels of my shoes were thick, solid.

"Oh," I said. "I like being big."

The two boys in the front shrugged and nodded at each other as if such a possibility had never occurred to them but might seriously be okay. Somewhere to the side, a girl with plump cheeks smiled up at me.

I watch Grosse Pointe Blank *again. The depressed hitman, dressed in a charcoal suit, stands near the steps of his former high school campus and runs into his former English teacher, arms filled with papers and books. The brick and glass edifice looming behind them could pass for a sanitarium. They chat.*

"You still inflicting all that horrible Ethan Frome *damage?"*

"No, Martin. It's off the curriculum now."

I watch him smooth his tie, wince a smile. I know there's a gun under his jacket.

I wouldn't have damaged you, Martin, I think to myself. I am still here, teaching at the school I graduated from, folding myself into the strange center of memory as students fling themselves away, forget it was all too real. I know why you left town on prom night, why you wanted to kill people. If you had been my student, I would have understood. You're doing a pretty good job for yourself in this movie, doing pretty well confronting virtual orphanhood, your hands dirty with murder, the love you tried to bury. In real life, maybe I could have saved you a lot sooner.

During my seventh year teaching, I find I am addicted to trash crime fiction. Something about the violence washes over me, seems natural now. First, one by one, John Sandford's series: Eyes of Prey, Mind Prey, Naked Prey, Rules of Prey. *Then J.D. Robb:* Seduction in Death, Reunion in Death, Witness in Death.

I don't remember plot details or specific cases — only that her eyes were gouged out, she was bound and gagged in the basement for forty-eight hours, she was raped repeatedly, her throat was slit, her hands were cut off, she was stabbed in bed, she was walking to her car, she met a friend at the library, she was successful, she was competitive, she was sexy, she was mousy, she was a homebody, we've never seen anything like what he did to her, the weird part is how she never mentioned his abuse before, the weird part is how no one believed her when she said she was worried for her safety.

My favorite series, the J.D. Robb series, takes place in the future and the detective is a female who kicks ass. I gobble these novels until they spill out from shelves and onto the floor. Then I stack them in Macy's bags and place them in a closet.

As a student in one of my 11th grade literature classes, Brian began with a passionate and lucid essay about the dark side of America's "city on a hill." Then, after receiving high marks and praise from me, he retreated into a sullen, apathetic presence in class. It was as if the moment I had recognized his work as "excellent," he darted back into himself, like a startled sea anemone.

One morning he sat with his arms crossed, staring me down, saying nothing when I asked him a question during the vocabulary lesson. I always kept this a low-stakes, interactive, and essentially playful exercise, allotting plenty of time for students to put sentences together before anyone was called on to share.

I waited. I wanted to acknowledge the resistance, then push into it. "Okay, okay. But what do you *think*?" I nudged some more. "Just try."

A skinny shrug. A scowl watching me watch him.

"You don't really want to do this," I said. I waited, then pressed my tongue up under my front teeth and moved on to someone else. I felt as if I had failed in some way—foolish—and that made me mad.

When I called him back at lunchtime, he burst open the heavy door and loped in, plunked down on a desktop nearby. His legs dangled towards the floor as I blathered something about how he needed to say what was on his mind, that classroom standoffs were a waste of our time and I wouldn't tolerate sulking.

He watched me as I gave my little speech, his eyes wide and sad like blue yolks. I could hear the industrial clock click to the next minute. Why so loud, that particular minute? I wondered. Then he nodded once, slipped from the desktop, and left, silent and resigned, the way he had entered.

The next day, and sporadically for days after that, Brian lingered after class, waited with his arms crossed on his desk, his back to me, as other students filed from the room. Sometimes he brought me a poem, either waiting for me to read it right then or leaving it on the corner of my table. The poems were usually unpleasant, even violent. One traced the step-by-step movements of a killer to the doorstep of his female victim asleep in bed.

I stepped lightly, attentive and uncertain in his silences what the real messages were—what, after all, is the line between artistic expression and real choices? I was both flattered and afraid. "This is bothersome," I would say, looking down at Brian's words in black felt tip pen. "This is raw. What else are you writing? Let's see something else, something about life."

He said next to nothing when he handed me pieces of text, but I read whatever he gave me.

I brought him books—Ai, Charles Bukowski. *There are writers better and more disturbing than you,* I wanted to tell him. *What do you think of that?*

He handed back the Ai collection, *Vice,* one morning. His face seemed wiped clean by a new expression. "Scary shit," he said.

"Yeah," I said. "She doesn't mess around." I handed him a paperback copy of Nick Hornby's *High Fidelity* as a bit of an antidote.

Brian started showing me a journal of poems and reflections he was composing with a female correspondent, a plain-looking three-hole notepad with a black cover. I hesitated, but accepted when he offered that I take it home. I stowed it in my roller bag for a few days before even looking. Inside were diary entries and lyric poems about "faeries," pencil and pen sketches, copied passages from favorite books, poems and song lyrics, unsettling descriptions (real or imagined?) of ritual self-cutting.

At the YMCA on school nights, I would pump my legs on the Stairmaster for forty guilty minutes at a time, try to lose myself reading a novel or listening to music on my cassette player. I worried that Brian was on a track to hurt himself, hurt me or someone else, worried that my approach was vain and selfish instead of compassionate.

"You know," I said to him one day after class, "when you show me disturbing things, I can't consider them purely confidential? You understand that I'm worried about you?"

I approached a male administrator and waited for something bad to happen, waited for a lashing, some indication that Brian felt betrayed. Instead, not long afterwards, his girlfriend flagged me down in the hall. "Thanks for being so nice to him lately," she said. "He really needs it. He appreciates it."

I started seeing him laughing in the hallway with her or slumped against one of her shoulders. He started popping by my room for a quick hello. In class, I watched him engage other students in conversation and spirited, yet not unfriendly, disagreement over quotes I had written on the board.

The following year he was a senior and no longer in any of my classes. In the school newspaper, when members of the graduating class name teachers who impacted them "for good," I found two sentences about me from Brian: "She gave me a flicker of hope that I won't be swallowed up by mediocrity imposed by our society."

It was jarring. I had no precise idea how or why things had turned for the better instead of the rotten. I had paid attention, though, and had probably been more of a witness than participant. We were still alive.

Two years later, one evening after dinner during the "honeymoon" period in the first month of school, I sat at the dining table where papers had replaced a meal. I wanted to knock off a stack of fifty short quizzes from two honors level classes, and I had a beat going: one point for spelling, one point for usage, slash, slash, total. I clipped along in a stride that felt like progress. Most students earned eighteen or nineteen points out of twenty. I had hit several perfect papers — great. The kids and I were new to each other. The clockwork rhythms were smoothing out.

Then the bump.

It actually took a while to register the content in front of me. I first drew X marks through sentences on the page, but still wrote a score at the top as if this were any paper, any other day. Then I sat paralyzed at the table and stared down at the quiz as it drew me back again, pulled me out of long-cultivated immunities. At the top of the sheet, I penned a message which read later like a ridiculous note to myself rather than the student: *What are you DOING??* And under that: *Sorry!! Unacceptable.*

Here was what the student, Mark, had served up for me to bring into my home:

> The FBI was able to <u>corroborate</u> that John Doe, in fact, was the gay rapist known as the ass pirate that had victimized so many people in [our city].

> Mark realized he had the gift of <u>augury</u> when predicting where the ass pirate would strike next.

> We realized the <u>artifice</u> of John Doe's personality when we found drugs, alcohol, and explicit photos of men in his home.

With the details from the crime scene, we <u>deduced</u> that John Doe was the ass pirate.

John Doe showed his <u>Herculean</u> strength when victimizing little boys.

John Doe was very <u>scrupulous</u> in hiding his true identity as the infamous ass pirate.

I stared into the wood-grain pattern on the tabletop. The scratchy jags reminded me of a seismograph scrawl when it registers tremors— *Was this a 4.6 on the Richter scale? a 6.1?* In my teacher-guts, where instincts like enzymes were always burbling, I knew this paper was a dare tailored specifically for me.

I remembered that Mark had asked, prior to taking the quiz: "Is it okay if we use names of classmates in our sentences?"

I had bent to whisper back: "No, better not."

He had blinked *Oh* and leaned over his paper, tucking his elbows in against his chest as he wrote the tiny letters. Thus his use of "John Doe"?

Perhaps I had recognized the icky game even then but, underneath, memories of Brian had left me willing to absorb almost anything. But Mark had done much weirder, if not more directly hostile things than Brian. He had been rude once as a "performance" for the six other male students in his class, then skulked back between periods to murmur an odd apology. His eyes darted down to the floor, only rising to reveal a glazed-over distance. There seemed to be a chronic mismatch between his body language, his words, and the remoteness of his expressions. But because I believed that I had weathered similar inscrutabilities before, I gathered myself to face them again. I called him in to talk about his vocabulary quiz. Things had to get better.

By coincidence, I discovered another paper by Mark the next morning when reading district student writing assessments during an official on-campus grading session. Barely a page long, the text's tiny letters ticked tight across the lines without any cross-outs, smudges, or erasures. The persona of this page spoke of himself as a model student, reflecting on a previous year of "vulgar and crazy acts" and articulating an epiphany of "new" selfhood. His last lines were something about how humility and peace could purge inner turmoil and disturbances. It sounded copied from a self-help manual—a bizarre juxtaposition to the paper I had read the previous night at home.

When we talked at lunch, Mark explained that he had gotten "carried away" on his quiz. He claimed that he "thought it was okay" because earlier that week I had apparently passed over, without comment, some double-entendre from one of his male peers.

I stressed how disturbing the stunt had been. I said I was concerned about the schizophrenic counterpoints represented by the quiz and the essay. But I also emphasized that I was ready to believe the vocabulary incident was just a silly fluke, a one-time blip of stupid judgment to be forgotten.

"It's in your corner to show me," I told him. I tried to get him to look me in the eye. "I'll just pay attention, like any rational person, and take what you do at face value."

Mark stared back at me with his vacant expression, said "Sorry" in a blank voice, not "*I'm* sorry"—he didn't use "I" statements—and then leaned forward on his elbows.

"Um," he said, heels bouncing. "So I get no points then, no credit, on the quiz?"

Princess Diana's son, Harry, is accused of cheating on a written project at the prestigious Eton School in 2003. The graded work gets him into Sandhurst, an equally prestigious institution where he trains as a military officer. The teacher who comes forward with these allegations has already been dismissed from Eton. In her argument against "unfair dismissal," she alleges that the head of her department had harassed her into doing Harry's work.

Lawyers for the teacher bring forward a tape wherein Harry states that he did "about a sentence" of the writing. Spokespeople for Harry's father, the Prince of Wales, insist it is unfair for the lawyers to give the court this small portion of tape. They counter that the tape is disjointed in places and only partly audible.

As part of his public PR rehab, Harry goes to South Africa where he plays ball with black children while cameras are running. He holds an infant victim of rape in his arms.

"I'd like to send her money," he says.

A few months later, another firestorm: Harry shows up at a party dressed as a Nazi.

I scramble to jot notes about a news report: a girl is found gang-raped at a school ditching party. She is found battered and naked in an alley. The report insinuates that the victim and perpetrators are Hispanic. When cameras cut from the police to the principal at the girl's school, we see him seated behind his desk, hands folded across a closed notebook. He's dressed down — casual Friday? — in grey sweatshirt and green Izod collar. "We want our kids to make good choices," he says. "In this case, the bad choice was ditching school."

In the weeks that followed, Mark became more insidiously disrespectful. It was almost like I had tripped a switch that gave him special permission. He had crossed one rare line I had never thought to explicate in eleven years teaching — *please do not turn in vocabulary sentences which identify yourself with perpetrators of anal rape and child molestation* — but even after our conference he disrespected a guest speaker, a female counselor visiting to talk about college testing; repeated mock comments, like "I *love* this class!" real loud at sporadic moments during discussions; leapt out of his desk to switch seats randomly in the middle of lessons or group activities; pretended to work, then asked questions phrased to sound phony and draw laughs, especially from the boys.

I felt a clock ticking. Mark's deterioration culminated in a plagiarized essay (lengthy intercuts of lame exposition from *SparkNotes*). After being called to the office for that offense, he slammed into class among his friends and started in, blaring how he was "screwed" now. The late bell had not yet rung, and I knew I was meant to hear every word from where I stood across the room talking to another student about her work. I had explicitly asked the administrator in charge of discipline to not send Mark back to class because I had anticipated this drama. I wanted distance, space. I had hoped not to be ignored, but here we were.

It was already a scene as I moved from my desk to the doorway and called him from the room. After weeks of his disruptive behavior, I was tired of putting on the nice front. "'I've got more *Cliffs* and *SparkNotes* if you want them," I said. "Back in my desk drawer? You want some more?"

He advanced up the aisle, wide shoulders lumbering. "No. No thanks." He was loud, buddies staring. "And um, for your information, that's NOT plagiarism. *Plagiarism* is…"

"That's enough," I said. "Come with me." I was struck by the certainty of his voice, the menace in his pupils that dodged nowhere now, but fixed on me as if to announce: *You're a stupid bitch. You don't get to call me out.* Another dare, more bait, another performance. I felt myself drawn into some voyeuristic spectacle, some dominatrix fantasy. Forget it, I thought. I'm going to act like a normal civilian — not some plastic "teacher" with a pink gag in her mouth.

In the hallway, Mark raised his palms like a Christ figure. To anyone nearby, I imagine his motions exaggerated my refusal to keep away from him, and made me look more like the attacker.

"You don't get to do this," I said. Then I slipped, saying something that I'm sure simply fulfilled my transformation from prude to hysteric. "I won't put up with this shit in my room."

I felt starkly alone, in the wrong, and righteous. At that moment, even my most eloquent rhetorical flourishes or stoic silence would not have suddenly inspired his respect. I resented how administrative obliviousness had led to more bizarre contact with him when I had taken steps to prevent this. And I knew Mark would use the curse, cite and repeat it — proof of my "aggression" and his victimization. I resolved to affirm my use of the word rather than running from it. No more traps, I thought.

As a campus aide finally appeared and ushered Mark down to the office, I realized that I wanted him out of my class permanently, yet I knew he would want to stay, would want proof of victory and institutional permission to continue his pattern. *How could he take it to the next level? What would be more extreme?*

Odds were that he would remain unless I had administrative back-up. Mark was suspended for five days for his plagiarism, but a weirdly unsafe feeling plagued me. Within hours I was ill and, from home, in a thrashed voice, I pleaded with my principal to help. He confessed he had no idea what had been happening because the discipline administrator had not yet communicated the story. Feeling nauseous, I composed a summary of events, progressing from the obscene quiz to the blatant plagiarism, having to justify, justify, justify what was disturbing and seemed personal, why I was unable to teach with Mark in the room. He needed serious help I could not — and would no longer try to — provide.

The meeting took place at a long oval table in the principal's office. The principal and myself, two other male administrators, and a union representative were present. No counselor, no psychologist. Mark arrived with both parents — educated people, professionals. His mother was short but solid and reserved looking, with perfect posture. His father was slender and slim-wristed, and he walked with a wooden cane. Mark helped his father sit at the end of the table and hooked the cane on the back of his chair.

I stared into a framed image on the wall behind the principal's desk—Al Pacino, in *The Godfather Part II*, glaring from behind praying hands.

I thought of *Grosse Pointe Blank*, where the female disc jockey wonders aloud into the microphone: "Where are all the good men dead? In the heart, or in the head?"

Mark began his explanation: "There was a lot of hostility in the class." He threw this line away as if it were obvious and launched into whatever else I can't remember. Hostility? I dwelt on that, thinking of how the boys were outnumbered by girls in his section— seven to fifteen. Plus me. An increasingly common gender disparity in accelerated language and writing classes.

The principal sat listening with Mark's discipline folder in front of him. I could see a sheaf of pink sheets inside it, and the principal pulled out one after the other. "You called this teacher a dyke," he said. "This one, you spilled water all over his books and called him a faggot." There was more. Then: "But you sit here and act like you've been wronged?"

From his seat across the table, Mark mad-dogged me. His father said, "At the beginning of the year, you were the only teacher who called us just to introduce yourself. We know you are a good person." He paused. "We encourage you to keep him in your class, to prevent bad feelings on his part."

To prevent bad feelings on his part.

I met Mark's eye contact. "Even the way you look at me right now," I said, trying to dislodge something. "What's that for? Why do you think you can do that? What have I done to you?"

No answer. No softening. Just silence and more staring.

The principal finally stated that he would accept my request to remove Mark from the class because of his general history of problems. Clearly, the continuum of incidents in my class had not been enough to justify administrative action. I found myself perversely glad that Mark had an extensive record of aggression, and yet I worried that with his file he was allowed to stay on campus without substantive interventions. Though counseling was vaguely suggested, no promises were made.

Despite some momentary relief, things took a more unsettling turn. The following night, in the midst of grading a new batch of essays from another class, I received a call at home—a mother reporting how her daughter was concerned that Mark was telling friends he might harm himself, *and the girls are over there right now, and I think he needs therapy or medication,* and what did I think she should do?

I fought not to break down on my end of the receiver. I thought of abusive husbands who threaten to kill themselves if their wives leave, set limits, or take the children away. I was appalled by the woman's lack of awareness, my own enforced silence, the fact that my reputation as a "good person" was dragging me towards Mark yet again.

"I have a safety concern," I said, trying not to use too many words. "Helping him is a job for adults, not high school girls. I can't talk about this. Call the police."

The principal had issued a verbal restraining order at the end of the meeting, but a male friend drove me to school for a week after that phone call. I had been shaken by students before, but I hadn't been afraid to walk alone on the open campus. I never did so again.

As expected, Mark buzzed by my doorway, testing, yet I didn't feel I could report it to anyone. I feared I had caused enough trouble without being cast as a "paranoid."

I had believed removing him from my class would re-establish a climate of balance and safety. Ironically, because I was not free to discuss what happened when he disappeared, the gender tension increased and went underground. I sensed pressure and disapproval even from boys who might have openly claimed to dislike Mark just a few days earlier.

My perception of this hostility was validated in a creepy way at the end of the year. One day when I was absent, Mark ditched one of his classes and impersonated my student aide for the substitute teacher. No one told me except a solitary girl who came forward the morning I returned. She whispered and looked over her shoulder, even though we were standing alone together in the empty room after class.

She was the girl whose mother had called me months before, the girl who scrambled to rescue Mark when he threatened suicide on the internet. He had later repaid her with threats of a different kind because she stood up to him, protecting a female classmate from repeated, unwanted advances.

Other films: The day Mr. Holland retires, he's informed that the music program he's spent a career improving will be eliminated. He's escorted to an auditorium filled with smiling people of all ages. On stage: an orchestra of students and former students under a giant banner – surprise! – "Thank You Mr. Holland." The state governor, also a former student, takes a seat to play clarinet. Holland lifts the baton, his chest heaving under the grey cardigan. He looks out at the audience, at the face of his wife and son. He will direct the one piece of music he's completed since he started teaching. He does. The director's heavy hand suggests fulfillment here, not irony. We're supposed to cry. Cut.

A prep school boy in blue blazer climbs onto his desktop and stands there, calling out to Mr. Keating: "O Captain, my Captain!" Keating pauses on his way out the door. Other boys mimic the action, repeat the phrase. They are all white, crying or near-crying, some with hands folded over their crotches. One boy wearing horn-rimmed glasses smudges his nose with a handkerchief. The bald headmaster, his accent vaguely aristocratic, yells and waves his arms. Keating freezes in the doorway like a man in a catalogue – with his briefcase, his cashmere overcoat. He looks back. "Thank you, boys," he says, chin angling up. "Thank you." Bagpipes and synthesizers swell on the soundtrack. This is the most he could hope for. Cut.

Conrack (in a film you can't find anymore) drifts away on a river raft as students stand watching from the dock. He is pale and blond and they are all black — some with braids and cornrows, some with no shoes. Each of the girls wears a dress. Nearby, on a post, stands a phonograph. One student places the needle onto a record. After some static, Beethoven's Fifth Symphony blasts into the air, across the moving waters. The raft draws Conrack down the river and out of the frame. The students stand, motionless. And cut.

Funeral pyre after funeral pyre, we buy the vision of teacher savior, teacher victim. There is never resurrection for the movie messiah, only resignation — whether inside or outside school walls. Male teachers play the (female) victim, become the expected sacrifice: I am only... This is merely... I am replaceable... I will redeem them or die. *For eleven years, I teach here, at* my *alma mater,* the mother school. *I open myself to the beautiful and ugly accidents that come with each class of students.*

I become a bad daughter. I want something more than alma mater *will allow me. How do I explain the guilt of* choosing *to exit rather than being pushed away? There's no soundtrack to make the choice feel like bravery, and I'm not "playing" the girl — I was raised one.*

Months after school ended and I was no longer a member of the staff, I was amazed at how glibly a male colleague dismissed my lingering discomfort about the series of Mark incidents.

"Hey," he said, leaning back in a patio chair. He waved his beer. "All adolescent male rebellion boils down to one thing. Simple. It's 'kill Mommy.'" He smiled like this was profound analysis, a moment to relax. I thought of the hill we were sitting on here in the backyard. "Wait," I said. I looked past the swimming pool and metal fence, past the freeway far below and out at the horizon of bruised-pink twilight. I took a long drink of wine that would probably bring me a migraine in the morning. "You'd have a harder time with that conclusion if you actually had to stand in front of class with breasts every day," I said.

With nothing but a shrug, he took a pull on his bottle.

Brian rented a room in a house downtown and got a job working long hours in the kitchen at a local restaurant. One autumn evening he called after his shift, loped to our doorstep holding up a paper bag containing leftover desserts he'd made himself: a perfect crème brûlée, a raspberry tart. My husband and I savored the delicate treats, spooning small bites from the ceramic dishes. Brian draped himself over a chaise, shared new aspirations to take out loans for college on the east coast. We exchanged books as we had before and would again, sometime later—a comforting, occasional ritual for now.

Where was Mark? I wondered. What would he bring with him where he was going—how was he damaged, and whom was he blaming? Would he get help? There were new rumors about his drug use, parents kicking him from the house, more suicide threats made to another teacher, the next woman in line.

As I rinsed out the dishes for Brian to take back to his restaurant, I realized that they weren't perfectly clean. I knew they'd have to be scalded and dried in an industrial dishwasher. I wondered whose job it would be to lift them from the machine—who, if she were too eager, too young, or too harried, might blister her hands on the hot edges.

In eleven years, here is some of what I learn:

A student copies a Shel Silverstein poem and reads it to the class claiming that he wrote it. The teacher calls mom, who insists her son thought he had done the assignment correctly.

A teacher gives a student a single 15-minute detention for tardiness. The student doesn't show and receives a 30-minute detention. The principal summons the teacher for a parent conference. The mother sets in: "This woman rolls her eyes at my daughter. She harasses my daughter." The teacher removes herself from the room instead of sitting there. Afterwards, the principal shames the teacher: "I'm really disappointed in you," he says. "You really left me hanging."

A would-be valedictorian is caught — and admits to — stealing an exam from a teacher's cabinet. The principal states that she will forfeit the honor of speaking at graduation. When the parents clamor for "due process," she is allowed to speak anyway.

An athlete with a massive record of fighting on campus pulls out his penis in math class when the male teacher's back is turned. A female classmate reports it. No other students confirm her report officially, though there is widespread gossip about the incident. Administrators insist they cannot do anything. The teacher resigns. The girl leaves school. Within two years, the boy is locked up in Chino Prison.

A student in a front row is openly copying someone else's essay. She seems to understand when the teacher takes the paper, crumples it, and tosses it into a trashcan. But her father leaves multiple messages for the teacher that night at home. "Who do you think you are?" he yells. "I pay taxes! I pay your salary!"

A teacher reports student drinking and narcotics use during a school function. He suddenly endures subsequent accusations of sexual misconduct by one of the offenders (a male). The principal pulls aside a few students, questions them just to make sure: "Does your teacher have inappropriate contact with kids?"

A teacher returns a summer phone call from a university chancellor. The chancellor's daughter's grade of "C" is "devastating," her daughter's life now "ruined" forever. "You didn't do what you should have done," the chancellor tells the teacher. "What I told you to do. I thought we had a deal."

A teacher is threatened on the phone in the middle of the night after grade reports arrive home. A voice screams something about failing — how it was the teacher's fault. The screaming voice calls five times. Police officers discover her truck windshield smashed with a crowbar, skid marks in the street, all the way down the block to her house. "Hey," the officers say. "School's out. It's time for pranks."

At an upscale school in an upscale neighborhood, students distribute a newspaper called The Occasional Blow Job, *which prints anonymous articles about teachers. In one issue, they superimpose the face of a teacher over the naked, splayed body of a porn model. Some students leave threatening notes on the teacher's classroom door. Walking across campus, the teacher hears students calling at her: "Slut!" She procures a formal restraining order when the school won't intervene. A judge in the subsequent lawsuit vacates the initial jury award on the teacher's behalf, says that she isn't entitled to the same protections against harassment as employees who work with adults all day.*

Two student athletes compose scenarios addressing their English teacher by name in journals for class: "I will still plot your murder," writes one. "I will put a fucking bullet through your mouth," writes the other. According to news reports, the boys' families insist that these and other vivid statements — "I will superglue you to the wall naked and cut your feet off" — require context to be understood properly. They should also be sealed from public view. The teacher had promised she wouldn't read the journals and besides, says one father, the assignment had encouraged posturing and one-upmanship.

In an email, a teacher expresses his strategy of ignoring whatever disturbs him at school. He says he learned this lesson even after being shot in the head in a campus parking lot. Now near retirement, he talks and talks about how he has designed the perfect program to teach writing and reading. He always has students write about and discuss a quote of the day. His long emails can't say enough about how he changes students' lives forever.

In / Out

You drop out early — as student, as teacher — for the same reasons you drop in: You feel cheated or think you're going to be, or you already lack something and want better opportunities. What else can you do with dread, with anticipation? The compartments and distinctions proffered by your father no longer serve, or serve too well. Silence has accumulated like water in your lungs, or else words borrowed from other people fill your mouth and gag like terry cloth anyway. Consent is barely the half of it — this is all about compulsion, about you needing to shake nettles from your shoes. Long accustomed to rhythms of dismissal — how a head turns away, how the bell blares transition — you have tired of being bullied. Mostly, you sense the bully inside yourself, how she smoothes her coat, fishes inside the shiny black purse where she has stored pretty things for protection and survival. You realize it's time to get serious, enter into other kinds of contracts.

You are haunted.

Remember: The boy stands up in his business class on the day you are just another nerd eating granola under a shallow-rooted tree. You are thinking about writing a paper on *Cyrano* and wondering how exercise could make your calves shapelier. It happens in the one classroom that has carpeting: He stands up after the Pledge of Allegiance and slips the gun (from his pocket? from his backpack?) against his own cheek. He pulls the trigger as if yanking a shock of hair out from the roots — one hard tug that people can only gape at, at first, like they have to make sure what is happening. Announcements keep blaring across the P.A. system, and the teacher — *why in her class? why with this group of classmates?* — she is still checking names on the roll sheet, fixing a typewriter and scribbling a pass to the health office. A girl has been asking, "Can I have some aspirin?" So much intersects in one moment. You don't hear the explosion — not even the people in the room hear the explosion. All the blood and skin pieces that had just been a person smack apart awkwardly across desks and attached plastic seats, on the arms of a nearby boy and girl, on somebody's PeeChee folder. Across the low-pile carpet, too, which has been industrial brownish-blue for twenty years. Afterwards, men rip the carpet out in strips so that the nails pop from the floor and crusts of dried glue remain visible on the slab. *Do they bury the carpet? Burn it? Toss it into a dumpster near the parking lot?* The door is bolted, computers and keyboards left for storage. Students and teachers let words sneak out of them after all this: *At least it didn't make national news, Thank God or nature it didn't happen in front of me, How sad* and *Shhh... How disturbed he must have been.* His classmates get pulled aside for a few hours by the county psychologist wearing khaki pants, the teacher leaves a year later, gets out of there — *not because of that,* people say, but because she wants some new sanity.

Her new sanity is real estate, divorce, remarriage, a baby. Your life doesn't stop that day, either. You write your paper on *Cyrano,* then another on *Brave New World,* then *The Stranger,* and so many other forgettable things. Sitting on the side of your bed at night, you repeat the calf-raising exercises that never make any difference. Why would the adults call together any general assembly for grieving, for finding another way to say the word for what one single, sad boy did to himself? You attend another school-wide anti-drink-and-driving assembly, apply to work on the editorial staff of the newspaper, dance the 80s two-step with friends when the principal puts new Coke and snack machines in central parts of campus. And there's prom.

Then the years of not-prom that are just real life. You feel the tug, the undertow, move along the mobius loop, knowing that rejecting what might absorb you makes you part of something similar. The principal at the school where you teach, the school where you were a nerd twenty years ago — where you are still a nerd, but with better clothing — he says an angel must have been watching over the campus, an angel who made it possible that the kid chatting up girls about guns on the internet got busted by the FBI after midnight. The kid emailed his idea to "do something" with a gun at school and luckily someone tipped off the authorities, or luckily the authorities were watching (no one is precisely sure which was the better part). The principal apologizes that staff and parents had to hear about the arrest on Friday night's TV news, and in the paper Saturday morning, then in the paper on Sunday. He doesn't say he's sorry that students didn't know what was going on, but maybe because that's because he knows they already did. Anyway, he wasn't here when the other kid actually *did do it*, when it didn't make national news, and looking around the room you realize there are a few people who were here, who were teachers here themselves when you were just a kid, but they sit blank as you. The day the principal talks about the angel is the day you notice his teeth look like plastic, expensive plastic teeth that might be purchased in a single piece. He adjusts his weight on the desktop where he sits, leans forward as if getting intimate with the small group and his body makes a roll under the black fabric just above his beltline. Strange intimacy, four days after the fact. Strange intimacy without come-to-Jesus questions like, *What doors are broken? Who do we call for help? Do you know, I was scared?* It is ritual enough to thank the nameless angel for his blessing. We deserved it. The boy is some kind of blight, some kind of Martian. You ask a colleague, *What is the name of this boy? Who is this boy?* And she says that as a professional she shouldn't tell you, as a professional she needs to keep his identity secret. You could not possibly understand or respect him. Knowing his name, knowing anything about him, would be the equivalent of gossip and that is all. He isn't your student, he isn't your own kid or one of your friend's kids, he doesn't belong to you. He's locked down now, locked away from his uncle's home arsenal — really, only a single wood cabinet, locked and loaded with weapons. The boy is protected from narrative, from anyone's memory, and there's no point dwelling on what he didn't do to us. Where was his angel? Maybe his angel wore a flak jacket and helmet, pointing his own weapon and kicking down the door? Regardless of all that hocus-pocus, you may wonder what color the boy's hair is, how close it's cut to his head, and that's fine as long as you keep it private. There's no sense dwelling on what isn't real, no sense being morbid or imagining what could stick like red Jell-O all over the insides of your hands.

These ghosts are orphans, really—one dead, one half-dead—and everyone else seems to know that. You are arrogant to think you might adopt them now, remember them, hear anything they might have to say. You leave school or step in thinking you'll fix things because you can't tell hypocrisy from lies anymore. You hear politicians and public planners talking about an abandoned, once-luxurious hotel and arguing it should be demolished and restored as a new campus—a fortress with hundreds of rooms and windows and a marble floor, perhaps, in the front lobby. It's an honor Bobby Kennedy was murdered there, because Bobby Kennedy was important and he stood for things, and the actual spot where his body fell can be preserved with a memorial plaque. There can be a dedication ceremony with black and brown children playing in a band and of course the building can be named Bobby Kennedy High School. His own son's public resistance to the idea just isn't practical, doesn't take into account the fact that we've just got to fix things *right now.* It's so much cheaper to remake the hotel than to build new structures in the city. What a dramatic tribute to history. Such a school can house four thousand students, organize and manage them in smaller units, called "academies," inside the massive institution. There can be principals in each academy, pointing visitors to shared spaces: *This is our pool. This is our counseling wing. This is our computer center, our library, our science lab. Here is where they shot him.*

Bunkers, Cysts

We lived, as usual, by ignoring. Ignoring isn't the same
as ignorance, you have to work at it.
— Margaret Atwood, *The Handmaid's Tale*

My first years teaching, I have it easier than most novices, although not in any way I might have imagined or predicted. Before graduating from college, I indulge the common fantasy that my world will be wildly expansive. I dream of leaving California after graduation, relocating to the east coast for a big signing bonus at a tough school in Massachusetts or Delaware. But I have no money, no car, to go anywhere. The local Nissan dealership offers one of those no-payments-for-three-months-if-you-prove-you're-hired-in-your-certificated-field deals for grads, so I snatch up the first job available: an English position at my former high school, only four years after leaving its hallways.

Despite the initial letdown of staying in town, I realize quickly that this contract means I won't have to learn survival as a new grown-up in an unfamiliar environment, among strangers who ignore me. I have a solid academic reputation to exploit, as I had been a fairly faithful, book-carrying, and obedient student—with only isolated moments of "saltiness," as one of my male teachers used to chide me. I know most of the faculty, know how to find bathrooms, the library and cafeteria, offices for discipline and attendance. By all superficial accounts, my *alma mater* remains "the good school" in town. What more could anyone want?

The month before classes begin, my mother nudges me from the nest, helps me move my twin bed, makeshift desk, bureau, a ghastly orange velour chair, and a single card table into a modest place just five minutes' drive from the school. I worry about rent before paychecks begin. "We'll loan you the money," my mother says, patting my hand. "Pay it back when you can." The apartment is a small, flat-roofed 1920s bungalow with big windows providing a view across a eucalyptus ravine, past the community college parking lot and street, and into the distant foothills. I stack books on the floor, cook macaroni from the blue box, plant pink impatiens and yellow marigolds in pots outside my front door.

My sole sibling is still a student—a senior—at the school when I start teaching. One day not more than three weeks into the school year she tracks me down—my sister who has always been the smiley one, who wears her straight, brown hair past slender, strong shoulders. We stand together near a drinking fountain that could easily pass for a urinal.

"It's Dad," she says, trying not to cry. "He left last night. Mom was screaming." She tells me about the slammed screen doors, my mother's fist pounding on the wall, her hands gathering pictures and lighting them into a trashcan on the back lawn.

My sister goes on to her next class, perhaps for an exam, a newspaper deadline, a lab report. I return to my classroom, the next group of kids, the next lesson plan. I want to make it matter that my principal frequently and supportively visits my classroom, tells me that I have "an unusual presence" with students, that he knows I can do my job, that I am suited for it. My colleagues seem mostly kind and chatty, and there's a constant mix of energizing students. Still, an isolation creeps in, a kind of grieving underneath. I think of my mother, of what's happening to my family. My mother, a teacher as devoted to other people's kids as she has been to my sister and me, now finds herself discarded after twenty-seven years of marriage. How can her sacrifices, her fidelity, come to this?

Still, I'm young and new. I trust in transparency, believing that my students want to know me and each other as much as I want to know them. The future lies in the future. "Education" isn't simply reserved for inside the walls. My classroom, like most, has no windows, so I've stapled up massive sections of blue paper on the long bulletin boards, tacked down a wavy yellow border along the edges. I hope the space will be brightened, *opened*, a little. One whole board, "The Write Stuff," I reserve for student work, their words, so at first it's mostly blank, like a wall of sky or water. On smaller square boards at the front of the room on either side of the chalkboard, I mount an erasable calendar, tack up snapshots of friends and family, center a giant poster of Penguins hockey star Mario Lemieux and, from *Life* magazine, a close-up of Princess Diana's face — notable because it had been doctored to show giant tears in her blue eyes. Colors and faces, I figure, human touches.

Another addition, the one I think most important, I place atop a cabinet situated near the door. Someone before me had painted the cabinet blood red, a hand-me-down I didn't think of rejecting. There I place a box — an old detergent carton I had wrapped in blue paper, with cut-out letters spelling M-A-I-L in diagonal along the front side, under the flap.

Dressed in a blue and white sailor-striped pantsuit and looking out at student foreheads and eyebrows and shoulders, I pick up the official curriculum binder, hold it open and say: "These choices have been made for you. These are the books we're supposed to read. This list didn't just fall from the sky." I tell them every word, every list, every symbol is a sign of someone's priorities, that I am committed to reading and understanding their own signals, hearing who they are — and what, looking around the room, can they tell about *my* values?

"You can't match colors," one girl calls out, and the class laughs. Other voices generate the obvious: I like hockey. I keep my schedule of days in some kind of order. I plan on having them write a lot.

"How about the mailbox?" I tilt my head towards the red cabinet. Bodies shift backwards in creaky desks. "What does that tell you?"

The blue box looks lonely and out of place. No one says anything, so I find myself explaining how I want them to ask for help privately if they prefer, communicate anything they feel better writing down rather than saying in person. By the end of that day, there's one note: loose-leaf paper folded into a tight origami bird with a long beak. In blue ink, someone has written: "This is neat. You're really creative. See ya tomorrow, Alex."

That one hopeful connection helps me look beyond the slurry of candy wrappers, gum wads, and sexually obscene questionnaires that find their way into the box. I figure it's worth acting as if I'm unfazed, unhurt. But one day, as students jostle out the door, a tow-headed boy grabs the box and kicks it down the hallway into a stairwell. I imagine the side of his face forming a snide laugh for a buddy as he leaves that crushed thing in a corner at the bottom of the cement stairway. I retrieve it myself, carry it upstairs against the tide of kids pressing down to their next classes. Not wanting to look at it anymore, I shove the mangled box into the grey trash bin beside my desk and feel myself pull inward just a little, storing a small piece in reserve. My older, wiser self knows the boy may be testing me, that he may want me to push harder for openness and authenticity in a place where sincerity is commonly mocked. But in the moment I sense my own limits intensely, feel that strange shame in being vulnerable. Some first thread of my teacher self shrivels up in a tiny corner of my most hopeful being, and twists into a tiny knot. The cement and plaster seems everywhere, around all of us.

Another class of students bustles to their seats before the final bell. Am I pretending to blow my nose in a tissue, just so I can cover my face? I think of my sister, soon graduating and leaving for college, my father yelling at me on the phone, "Two girls at university – and what do I have to show for it?" My mother, leaving early for her own egg-crate school each morning, knowing she'll return all too soon to an empty house.

Back in the real moment, a voice: "What happened to the mailbox, Ms. Scott?" A boy saunters through the doorway and chomps gum as if he knows all too well.

"Oh…" I say. I feel for a book on a shelf inside the lectern another student has painted and decorated — a lectern that says, in flashes of black and blue, *Shun Those Studies in Which the Work that Results Dies with the Worker.* I open the book on an empty desk at the front of the room. "That mailbox thing isn't going to work out anymore. Not right now."

The last few students barge in, loud and sullen and cheerful, preoccupied with gossip and plans, unshifting backpack straps from their shoulders, fiddling with folders. Someone still eating a candy bar.

Like a needle on a record with indelible scratches, I skip on to the next groove — the next lesson plan, the next stack of papers to grade, the next test to write, the next parent meeting. I go on as if I don't mind teaching in a cell, pretend not to notice the slow pull of forward motion into smaller and tighter circles. Years later, a woman ready to retire will put her hand on my forearm when we talk about something violent students have done to a colleague's house. "You build a cyst around those things," she says. "It's the only way to survive."

While the students come and go, I don't leave this room for stretches of four and five hours at a time. The cinderblock walls become like arms, holding me blind. *Is it raining? Has there been a fight down in the courtyard? Are visitors strolling the campus today?* The isolation becomes real once I am truly hunkered down inside. One day during the middle of a lesson — students in their desks, writing in journals — we have an electric blackout. Capital "D" darkness hits. The kids squeal. I can't find the regulation flashlight, or do I have one? "We can do this, guys," I say. I work my way to the door, prop it open to the dark hallway, where other classroom squeals and teacher voices are echoing as if through a sewer tunnel. I edge across the hall to the faculty lounge, prop open its door so a small window can cast us a swatch of grey shadow. We are glad to settle for it. We tell ghost stories.

An outsider might say the confinement for teachers is voluntary, that I don't have to be here unless I really want to be confined. That if the walls are bad for students, they might be good for me. I get used to staring at the sheetrock and plaster and bricks, the glare of fluorescent light on white-boards, grey file cabinets, banged-up Formica desks and table tops, scuffed tile under foot, drop-ceiling drywall with water and Freon stains. We need to be focused, says the literature on schools, we need standards and productiveness. A worker mentality.

We fear vandalism—or we believe vandalism is inevitable. Perhaps a teasing window is soldered shut permanently, a façade nailed on outside the window cheats the view. Such design can become a force in itself, inspire desire to smash things, if only to smash through.

I gather a few students to paint one whole wall at the back of the room bright blue. We chat up plans to add things: quotes from writers, faces, maybe a giant sun. The students graduate before the mural can be completed and I stay behind with my blue wall. I like the swatch of permanent color, how it doesn't fit anything else in the building.

I flatten one hand again against the blue wall, and then remember: just cold.

I'm at a party for a new baby, a child whose years of school lie far ahead of him. Across the reception table, beyond the cake and quiche and sliced ham, a contractor talks about his experiences doing jobs for a school district. I cross my legs and listen.

"This one woman—this *teacher*," he says. "She was holed up in a back closet as a makeshift office. There was a sewer line right under the electric cord. Her computer on a card table. I told her, 'Hey, you just can't be here.' Getting her out of there held up the whole project for days."

Time adds up for any teacher in the bunker. Staying alert and on guard in a closed environment, anticipating to protect one's students and one's self from harm, strips something from you. Even at your best, you aren't at your best. At teacher meetings, I look around the room of mostly women, their smiles wired so tight and invincible, and I know something about what the mask of okayness covers. Why do we, like our students, feel obligated to deny our need for light and fresh air?

Years go by. I am department chair. The second day of my two-year term, an administrator pulls me aside in a gossipy whisper. "You really need to do something about Mrs. Ryan," she says. "The woman's wacko, totally losing it." Supposedly, Mrs. Ryan, a longtime professional, had broken into tears that morning and stepped for a moment from her classroom.

"I've done that before," I say. "My students survived. What was she supposed to do?"

Overhearing us, another veteran teacher pipes in, her voice over-loud and sure of itself. "Well," she says, her tone perfectly modulated to punctuate the point. "I've *never* cried. I've *never* broken down."

In fact she had been barely able to express her anger at something that had happened the previous school year. Two male honors students were caught stuffing nails and screws into her car tailpipe, and she was urged — by the same teacher whose emotional balance was now in question — to press for disciplinary consequences beyond a mere slap on the hand.

Maybe the cysts become so large, so impermeable that they detach us from "normal" human reactions outside school walls: outrage, grief, joy. Like a build-up of drugs or alcohol in the system, the cysts can make people oblivious to wounds for long periods of time. Waking later, after a long sleep, one wonders where the flesh-gouges came from, and why there is blood on the sheets. But if we catch someone else expressing what we can't, we're trained to be offended.

A new teacher tells me one evening on the phone how she "went off" on two young men. They had openly and loudly mocked a classmate with a stammering problem as she struggled to complete a poetry recitation in front of class. When the teacher saw tears in the girl's eyes, she couldn't take it anymore.

"I told them to get out, into the hall," she tells me. "And when the girl finished, I went out there and just lost it. I was so angry... Tomorrow, I'll have to apologize."

"Wait," I say. "You were *moved*. Don't you think they needed to see your reaction?"

I wonder aloud if those two students have ever seen an adult so affected by their abuse of another person. I tell her not to take back the emotion or couch it in apologetic terms. Shall we train our students to see that there is no middle ground inside us, that there's nothing between the basketcase and the stone cold professional? Shall we pretend we are made of cement, like the walls we try to hide with colored paper, or with paint?

Sometimes, you try to speak. One teacher who takes her class to the gym for a school-wide alcohol awareness assembly notices that the students and faculty are crammed in everywhere. Half of the bleachers are still tucked in, so students must stand and sit wherever they can. All the exits are blocked by bodies. There's nowhere for teachers and some latecoming students to sit down.

She emails the director of activities, who brushes the concern aside. She emails the principal: *You'd think someone would give a damn about safety.*

The principal doesn't respond. Instead he summons her, this tidy woman with a soft voice who used "damn" for the first time in twenty years of campus correspondence, into his office. "Sign here," he says, sliding a sheet of paper towards her angular hands. "I'm writing you up for profanity."

———

One late afternoon, a teacher friend and I meet up in a restaurant. We find ourselves seated at a U-shaped booth next to another U-shaped booth where a man sits quietly lecturing his wife. Most other tables are empty, so we hear him, and her silence, too clearly. Perhaps it's a minor disagreement that only sounds mean, something about the name of a vegetable, or a dessert she shouldn't be eating. We recognize his wife, sitting quietly with her chin down, hands under the table. She doesn't look at us and we tuck our foreheads down behind open menus. She is a colleague, a longtime veteran who runs her classroom as if she is master and commander at the far end of the world.

By the time the waitress arrives, our friend is slipping out of the booth, following her husband, leaving without a word.

"Weird," my friend says.

I take a long draught of my own black coffee, and we spend the next two hours venting about our own problems with students, administrators, and men.

Not long afterwards, the colleague in the booth is promoted to work at the district office. In the months before getting this job, she weathers one of the chronic scourges of teacher life for the last time. I first hear about the incident in a morning class, from a good kid who is feeling insulted — not by the perpetrators, but by this teacher.

"It's not fair," the girl says. She slams her purse and book bag and body into her desk that morning. "How can she punish all of us?"

Allegedly, a T.A. in an Advanced Placement class stole an answer key for a final exam and made it available to all the students. The teacher forced herself to create a different test and made all the students retake it.

The incident is the final demoralizing stroke in a long and successful classroom career for this woman. The cysts — of isolation, of denials — have grown too big, can no longer be concealed, have leaked too much poison into her system. I notice that she doesn't smile and speak in the high-pitched, vapid voice of the many who claimed to be "just fine" with everything. No more cheerleading. Time at last to see the stains on the bunker ceiling.

On one of her last days on campus, I bump into her in a counselor's office, a tiny square room with two doors standing open on opposite walls. As usual, her tailored clothes, haircut, and nails reflect style and care. There's an impeccable gold necklace at her throat. We chat about the new opportunities she faces, talk about ways we handle and channel stress. She tells me she has done needlework for years — knitting or crocheting, I can't remember which.

"I cook," I say.

She shakes her head, mouth and brow melting into parallel, grim lines. "Cooking disappears," she says. "It doesn't last."

I follow her logic in my head: Furniture layered with knitted afghans, crocheted pillows mounding in every corner of every room like soft boulders, bedspreads, handtowels, cross-stitch designs pulled tight and mounted into frames, window drapes, Kleenex box covers and mantelpieces and placemats. Something, maybe, for each well-loved student who has spun away from her, for each loss she blames on herself, for every parent conference gone sour, each lesson plan failed or aborted in twenty-five years of teaching.

Perhaps filling in, too, for the last admission she makes, knowing how easily her words may transgress the bunker fantasy: "It's not good for me now," she says. "And it's the kids. I can't take the kids anymore."

Calling

It begins with impressions from books, church, music lessons — they form a kind of seamless caul that holds and draws you towards adulthood. A desire gestates here, this place that feels practical, connected to the dailiness of *May I? Can I?* and *Every Good Boy Does Fine.* (Does he really? You never stop wondering.) Teaching becomes merely one container inside another container made of writing and reading, melodies and dissonance, pictures of saints and imaginary friends. Words and notes as landscape seem natural, if not always comfortable, a place to inhabit — the way another landscape of numbers, photographs, proofs, or experiments seems natural to friends who choose surgery, the courtroom, interior design, plumbing, or selling cars.

A few first moments: Your parents give you a book with blank pages, bound as if it were already published. "A Nothing Book," your father says. The smooth paper sheets have no lines, and you begin to imagine a long story recalling other stories that have provided consolation. The martyr who laughed when men dragged her body across hot coals. The nun whose cheeks glistened onscreen as she wept and prayed. You are too young to know how white or how lonely you are, or what this would mean if you could talk about it. You do recall breaking into tears after swimming lessons, remembering the tufts of brown hair that appeared in a girl's armpit as she reached out one lithe, pale limb to draw a classmate from the blue water. It was rescue practice in case a person was drowning, sinking. Somehow it hurt that the girl didn't worry what others might see, that she had not been embarrassed by herself. You still envy her, wondering where that quality comes from. So on the blank book, using a salmon-colored crayon, you scrawl a title on the cover, something like "The Poor Family." Underneath, you draw what resembles a covered wagon and then cringe at how broken it looks, especially around the rickety wheels. You start writing then what you think you are allowed, permitted, a story someone else has already written — *Little House on the Prairie? A Christmas Carol? Nancy Drew's Mystery on Lilac Lane?* Already, this inner wrestling feels urgent.

As becomes habit, you drag fingertips across bookspines filling grey shelves along one living room wall, touch and wonder where these texts come from, how they are written and manufactured and make it to the grainy shelves. How *other* they feel, how alien you are, touching their seams. A soft sense of doom and resignation descends, as if you realize those books might suddenly plummet down, bury and smother you. As if there is conversation among these shelves you may not enter, you cannot enter. You overhear adults talking politics in a nearby room, voices loud and laughing, assured of their places, not worried about you under the avalanche of books, not worried about being swallowed up themselves. (You realize years later how this was a child's perception, how their worries, while different in details, were much about smothering and being smothered). You reach a small hand for the dictionary, look up a new word that has come to concern you — *masturbation.* Too young for euphemism, too young not to fixate, you stare down at the spelling, at the definition, wonder whether it helps to see the syllable and accent marks there, like science without sin, the surprising "u" in the middle instead of an "e." Your mother and father are among voices now clamoring new phrases that become intriguing: *curriculum, back to basics, the dangers of secular humanism.* You hear someone — your mother? — run water over glasses in the kitchen sink, perhaps the adults are moving into the living room now. You close the dictionary, slip it back into place, make yourself seem to disappear.

Nervousness underlies this need for meaning and sorting terms, sorting feelings, but there are comforts. At the small church school, you take part in a spelling bee in the church basement that smells of old marble, beeswax, cooking grease, and incense. The same basement where your parents fry doughnuts with other parents during fund drives in winter, where the Knights of Columbus serve pancakes and sausages twice a year, where families gather with their kids to play small time bingo or walk the cakewalk. In that spelling bee, in your plaid uniform, you advance to the local finals and don't win, but there is a teacher who encourages you. She seems nearly sixty years old, a German Lutheran who folds hands across her soft-looking waist and closes her eyes, moves her mouth to the words while the class prays together. She doesn't make the sign of the cross, but she prays the Hail Mary like it's her own prayer. Nuns visit the classroom from out of town (passing through from Boston? New York City?), strong but not strident in long habits swishing black against wood rosary beads. They smile, talk with you, open their briefcases and take out books they have published — on theology, the saints, prayer, the sacraments. You are not the only child who is impressed. The boys aren't so interested, but you hear other girls saying, "I could do that." Your father has even said something like, "You could do that." (He probably doesn't know about the masturbation.)

You wonder: where is the medium, where is the variation on a theme that fits my life? You can't forget the Lutheran teacher, who sits at the end of the fifth-grade pew each weekday before mass, an hour before school, waiting for students who straggle in. She kneels with everyone else when the priest raises the bread and wine. It seems that, to her, prayer is prayer. A word is a word is. Perhaps denominations are temporary, a mere abeyance. You think of the teacher those Sundays your father yanks you, yanks your sister and mother to the front pew, where he refuses to kneel at the moments everyone else is kneeling. He seems to be performing his act of not kneeling for everyone behind him. You're not sure if, like your mother, he even wants to be Catholic. In a weird way, you believe if he could just kneel you'd relax, you'd be able to speak better — and not just you, but your mother, your sister. Books might make sense instead of seeming like an avalanche, a tidal wave ready to drown you. There's something inside you that's always kneeling down, ashamed, even when you do things well.

But as friends learn piano on uprights that fit in corners of kitchens and living rooms, you begin on the oboe, a Bundy made of plastic. Parents pay for summer music lessons at a public school where you learn scales and old standards. (This is, really, a certain gift from your father. He has played trombone, piano, organ. He has introduced you to records: Dave Brubeck, Handel, Dr. Buzzard's Savannah Band.) Something in these lessons clicks you away from anxieties, away from the tidal wave. You've found a thread or electric wire, perhaps a vein. Perhaps your parents see some change in your face. No matter what concepts they imagine you may reject from them later — *back to basics, the fear of secular humanism* — they do feed this thing that lets you fly wherever. They sign the blue checks from the bank. A note is a word is.

The conductor of the city symphony takes on individual students. He's an oboist, but years-fluent with every instrument. Week by week, you follow the downslope of the auditorium carpet, quiet as church, to the side stairway that leads up past practice rooms and to his office, a kind of turret. His windows angle open to the trees and the evening, his desk scattered with sheet music, symphony scores and open books. You are a minor part at the end of his day, you are not afraid of him, you have, in some small way, chosen each other. You never feel unsafe in this room, alone with this man. Every wall is filled with shelves, which are teeming with record sleeves, cassette and eight-track tapes, books and concert programs. He begins with real music — a sonata by Telemann, a concerto by Bach. He traces a white finger under notes on the page. "Just listen right here," he says. He lifts a flute from where it lies across papers on his desk, eases it under his lips and dips his head into the breath he pushes through. "Do you hear how the notes go?" he asks.

How unworried he is that you possibly might be intimidated, that your small fingers certainly will flub and fail. His lack of worry makes it possible for you really to hear. To read. He gives you a recording to take home, a real musician performing, and he tells you to practice by ear. It doesn't matter that your instrument is made of plastic, that Telemann and Bach are so absurdly far beyond the reach of your current preparation. The notes are letters, a language carrying you beyond what you will be expected to say.

Teaching and expression crash together here, in this place you've felt distinctions erode. You intuit, and then you think, *There must be others who want this safety.* There's no warning—not from mother or father, not the dictionary or German Lutheran teacher, not the nuns who visit or the conductor with his flute. You don't wonder for a second how to name this awareness, whether it will be useful or become outdated, or how it will translate. This is you and way beyond you. The gift won't simply become the classroom or the grades you record in a tidy line across graph paper. It's not about old books toppling from shelves, or Formica desks, or announcements across the public address system or memos from the principal. It doesn't matter how as a grown-up you will simplify this vocation at times—talk about getting paid too little or too much—and it doesn't matter that politicians will pat you on the head (metaphorically, of course) in that coded way that warns, "Just relax, you hear me?"

Yours is no fall back plan, no second-hand profession. It's a kind of pregnancy you learn to carry, these nine-month increments of time coming to term—or not—in beats and measures, pages and paragraphs, from Fall through Spring. Words and flesh brush against, then become music to each other. Picture that girl's slender arm again, the "V" of hair opening as she offers herself perpetually to someone else across blue water. The person she reaches to either reaches back or doesn't. You can't always know. Remembering now: it was partly the offering that made you cry, the cheerful lack of agony inside her openness. Catching a hand, a breath, and *what if* slipping from the edge or watching a head go under, a drowning. It happens over and over, always the others: leaving, staying. They choose. You choose. The classroom door closes. You carry their names long after they forget how, once, you might have existed.

The Seven-Year Itch

I can feel their bright black eyes on us, the way they lean
a little forward to catch our answers…
"Yes, we are very happy," I murmur.
I have to say something. What else can I say?

— Margaret Atwood, *The Handmaid's Tale*

The teachers carry their purses, which contain their lipsticks and tampons,
compacts with and without mirrors, fruit and flower scented hand lotions
in smudged plastic bottles, gum in mashed packages, receipts, Motrin,
Band-Aids, the cell phone with programmed numbers: Kids, Husband, Ex-
husband, Parents, Mom's doctor, the Babysitter, the Handyman. Inside
their bodies they carry other things: arousal and bleeding, anti-depressants,
scars, incontinence, embryos, dead eggs, hormone serums, nicotine, alcohol,
Slim Fast. In their bodies lies a vivid memory of younger bodies, their own
student bodies. They carry that memory as if the younger body is more real
than the present one. If a strange man asks, a teacher will pull pictures from
her wallet: sons and daughters, grandchildren, nieces, a nephew, favorite
pupils, her own driver's license photo. If the man asks something yes or no,
the answer will always be Yes. Yes.

According to the National Center for Education Statistics (NCES),
thousands of public school teachers pack up boxes and roller bags
and walk away from their classroom desks every year. Commentators
wring their hands about the large number of new teachers who
depart within three years, neophytes who may look attractive simply
because they don't stay in the profession. We seem less interested in
what happens when the neophyte does stay, becoming just another
frayed veteran with so many years invested in her job, in other
people's offspring, that she may believe she has no other options
anymore, or that considering other options might seem actually

immoral. NCES reported in 2007 that teachers who stay past ten years are amazingly "cheery" in their claims of satisfaction on the job. But given the likelihood that such teachers will be women, such cheeriness seems both unsurprising and misleading.

I've heard longtime teachers confess, standing with a heavy canvas tote as students bump past them in a hallway, or staring into rows of potato chips and candy bars in a vending machine that just stole their change: "If I could leave, I would." They might joke openly of the desire simply to retire, to stop working, but the desire to stop teaching seems loaded with a heavier sense of personal, even ethical and perhaps gendered, failure. *Did I care enough? Did I give enough? Am I being negative?* I've overheard more than one woman colleague say, half-kidding, "Well, if I left, what would happen to the kids?"

Perhaps teachers themselves envy or resent "the ones who get away" because, well, they get away. In the ordinary household of just another campus, the shiny new bride eventually becomes mother-housewife. And mother-housewife is always haunted by the loose woman, the mistress.

Somehow, during the first seven years I taught among the colliding and sometimes brittle examples in the domestic order of things—at home? at school?—I learned how to be both kinds of teacher: the mother and the mistress.

Night. My dad shows up at the bungalow where I am just settled, a first-year English teacher. He sits near the desk where I stack papers for grading and keep the green, grid-lined logbook of student names, points, credits and deficits to tally. "I'm not buying furniture," he says. "That would be too permanent." But already I intuit a separateness: his balding head looks newly tan; he wears a navy-blue nylon jogging suit although, in two decades, I have never known him to jog. He refuses to leave address, phone number, any trace of contact information. He says he can't take it anymore. My mother never stands up for herself, tells him off. "I'm not Charles Ingalls," he says.

Charles Ingalls. Husband and father from Little House on the Prairie *books, immortalized on 1970s TV by Michael Landon: steadfast and broadshouldered prairie homesteader, the man no woman would ever want to leave. Ideal father for daughters who will become teachers, writers, homemakers. Working partner instead of glib patriarch.* I'm not Charles Ingalls. *The line gives my dad's departure an obvious logic, a cheap excuse. It implies something more difficult for me to bear: If he is so unworthy, so leavable, why did my mother stay with him?*

The answer comes in pieces. One hushed Sunday after the finalized divorce, my mother speaks gravely to my sister and me in a saggy vinyl booth at an IHOP. "Your dad has everything backwards." She doesn't lift her eyes from the table. She folds and unfolds a napkin in her lap. "Your dad wants to be happy. God wants us to be good."

In literature and composition classrooms, teachers often instruct by negative example. We test and practice, monitoring syntax and semantics to illustrate simple contrasts: Is this sentence correct or incorrect? Why? How would you fix it? Standardized tests, and even standardized test *practices*—with their blue or red bubble Scantron forms and multiple choice answers—sadly narrow the field of examples from which to choose. The multi-million dollar industrial test complex assures schools that this is the best way to track learning, and by year seven, any teacher is well-versed in this gospel.

Yet this gospel doesn't always assist in the complex work of generating sentences on the page, nor does it help create sentences in the social sense—as in life judgments or decrees. Life sentences. Sometimes the very students who perform best on error-spotting tests have problems articulating language or paragraphs of their own, out loud or on the page. The approach infects teachers' voices as well, employing a binary and agonistic answer key with an implied "right" answer: *Are you a good teacher or a bad teacher? A team player or a hold-out? A disciplinarian or a basketcase? A satisfied stayer or dissatisfied leaver?*

By this standard, "good" teachers are supposed to be drowned by the demands of their work lives, all for the good of the children. Any teacher who escapes this misery merely proves her capacity for self-indulgence—or witchcraft. It makes sense that in my own history of positive and negative examples, I have made impossible and false discriminations between "goodness" and "pleasure," "badness" and "misery," as if all were distinct as commas or semicolons on an annual test where no explanations are warranted. In my career as well as my personal life, I have sometimes clung to, or denied, what has hurt me as if it were the key to goodness—or the correct answer to somebody else's question.

Examples, I

From an early age, discomfort feels like something I must make familiar. As an eleven-year-old, I choose Maria Goretti for my patron saint at confirmation. Canonized in the early twentieth century, Maria was a young girl who suffered death by brutal stabbing because she refused the sexual advances of a young man who wouldn't take "no" for an answer. The murderer's eventual conversion to Catholicism in prison is attributed to Maria's holy, deadly resistance. He claims she appeared to him in a dream, arms brimming with white blossoms.

Maria is a perfect match for me because, in the way of sad and self-pitying children, I feel contaminated: by thoughts of cool and soothing mud across my breasts and genitals, by the sweetness of Oreo cream on my tongue, by a fear that my ankles will always be too thick for love. I want too much to read and know, to be never wrong—at least never to look that way.

Martyrdom offers one perfect example: the ultimate holy-card, a final trump, a fantasy of immaculate redemption.

In my seventh year teaching, one of my honors classes had too many students the first month of school. A loose-breasted woman administrator wearing a country-checkered dress visited us, declaring that four or five must volunteer to leave the class because of overcrowding. "Or else," she said, tapping the notepad cradled against her chest, "I'll have to pick people."

The students were openly incensed. "What do you guys want to do?" I asked. "Do you know the steps a student can take to speak up, to participate in the process?"

Many wanted to petition the school board. They composed individual letters, signing another collective letter written by a class representative. They elected two girls to present their documents at an official meeting. The night we showed up, the aisles were already packed with cafeteria workers, janitors, and secretaries thundering their shoes on the hollow floor to protest their own expired contract. One of our students, crisp in a professional looking jacket and fearless braces, gave her speech as the official timing bulbs burned green, then yellow, then red. The shoes thundered solidarity as she took her seat again.

Afterwards, in the vestibule, as she and her companion slipped arms into coats and whispered to each other, glowy-faced with accomplishment, the superintendent suddenly appeared.

"I'd like to come and visit you, visit your class," he said to us. The gestures of his stout body, the way he smoothed his tie, suggested nervous urgency, almost courtship. "I'd like to answer your questions in person."

A week later, wearing a full suit, he showed up. "Would you like to come to Sacramento with me?" he asked, leaning an elbow against the lectern. "To see how things get done?"

He followed through, taking several student representatives from accelerated instructional programs, along with a few teachers, on an ultimately pointless but politically positive daytrip to the capital. Afterwards, the district newsletter published a black and white photo from the journey: a few students, four teachers (including me), and the superintendent, all of us smiling together, hair wind-whipped on the leaf-strewn steps of the Capitol building.

Not a negative example, I thought.

Not everyone agreed. Whatever limited but positive effects for students, I had essentially cheated on the home administration. My principal chided me for going "behind his back" to welcome the superintendent into our class.

Examples, II

During Christmas break, shortly after my father disappears, I hook up with a man who seems a good match for me. He tells me he's twenty-five when he's really thirty-three, and I believe him. Because of an anxiety disorder, he often takes hours to lock or unlock his door — he slips and clicks the key, removes the key, thumps his tongue, counts numbers…slips and clicks the key, removes the key, thumps his tongue, counts numbers. I stand and witness for hours sometimes, silently, years before I understand. He shifts from job to job waiting tables. Since an accident that had torn the toes from one foot and much of the flesh behind one calf, he has stopped attending college and has stopped taking photographs. Now he keeps dusty old prints, negatives, rotten film, and expensive cameras in a side room with boxes of plastic-wrapped Playboys. He sleeps on a twin mattress with a giant hole heel-ground into the foam, exposing springs. He uses no mattress pad, no slipcover, no sheets, only a ratty chenille bedspread. He can't sleep overnight with me, or say I Love You, or engage in anything but sex of the oral/digital variety. I take seven years to learn how to leave him.

I was never sure I'd survive a whole career as a public high school teacher, but after my father left, as relieved by his absence as I might have been, deep down I wanted to be as little like him as possible. He had quit teaching to become a B-52 navigator for the Air Force, then quit the Air Force just three years before he could have retired, then taught elementary school again, then quit two days before school started and went into the mortgage business, then quit our family as if he'd never been part of it. Fairly or not, my father became the negative example of restless self-involvement, a sign of everything I thought I should avoid.

Still, conveniently, I had promised myself during university days that, if (when?) I tired out, I'd remove myself from the teaching scene to recharge, for however long was necessary, not just to preserve my own sanity but to protect my students. I'd known burnouts who stayed: chalk-stained and time-fried, disinterested and lonely, lecturing past student foreheads at the back wall, laughing at their own jokes, flinty or brittle in their claims of devotion to "the children" and strained or abrasive in their interactions among adults. Some seemed like starving and emaciated waiters at a chatty banquet table, people who coped by denying their own hunger, their own desires.

Ironically, in my seventh classroom year—the year that supposedly bodes wanderlust in marriage—I became more relaxed as a teacher precisely because I allowed myself to drift from teaching and relax into my life. For one thing, I hadn't seen or spoken to my father in nearly six years, and I experienced that loss as guilty liberation, a strange breathability. I fit back into the jeans I had worn at eighteen. I worked out on the StairMaster at the local Y every day and splurged on classy wool suits. Since I had just completed a Master's degree and no longer had thirty mile commutes to and from the college campus after school hours, I found other ways to pack my time after papers were graded: typing newsletters and press releases for Habitat for Humanity, launching a poetry series to raise money and attention for the organization. I attended Jack Grapes's poetry workshops in L.A., then published poems and read my work at venues like Café Luna, Midnight Special Bookstore, Back to the Grind. Every other Wednesday after school for a few weeks that seventh spring, I made the hour-or-so drive to Cahuenga, off Sunset Boulevard in Hollywood, simply to pick up bins of submissions to read for *Caffeine,* a small but well-circulated coffeehouse lit magazine. I even made quiet peace inside my dead-end relationship. I felt grateful, actually, that the experience was teaching me how to survive alone.

Such promiscuity stretched time outside class deliciously thin, so that in my own body, by year seven, a contradiction was growing. I wouldn't have predicted that developing confidence would inflame rather than subdue classroom exhaustion or sensitivities to bureaucratic demands, but restlessness lingered as I realized my classroom was only one part of a larger and more coherent picture. One question was still forbidden: *Could I choose not to teach for a while – simply because I didn't want to teach for a while?* There were no ready examples I could turn to for reassurance. Every teacher I knew was still teaching for dear life.

Examples, III

In year seven, my girl students swoon over James Cameron's romantic blockbuster, Titanic: *how the main character boards the ship resigned to marry a man who doesn't respect her, all to save her widowed mother, and herself, from destitution; how in fact her life changes within hours all because the right man stumbles across her path. And then he sinks into the sea.*

A colleague and I wait to see the movie until it lingers at one last local hole-in-the-wall. Two or three people sit isolated in dark rows behind us. We prop feet on the seats in front, snicker at all the wrong places for the first hour of the melodrama. But then we see the iceberg – the one we already knew was coming – rip the underside of the ship like a piece of aluminum foil. We watch the unsuspecting passengers continue to play cards, clink cocktail and champagne glasses, dance and argue, have sex, and tell jokes. Before general panic strikes, an isolated few move calmly to the lifeboats. The man who designed this model cruiseliner, this ship that could never sink, realizes with guilty eyes that, counter to his instincts, an inadequate number of lifeboats have been attached for the maiden voyage. The captain locks himself inside the helm and waits for it to become a death chamber. I tense back into the seat cushion and can't stop thinking that if the me of the last seven years had been a passenger, she wouldn't have fought to get herself off the ship.

A new teacher arrived at the school that seventh January. He had lean legs and thick shoulders, wore a battered leather jacket, Doc Martens and metal-framed spectacles, carried an old-fashioned hard-shell briefcase every day. Fresh from earning a Master's degree in England, he had no teaching experience yet.

This teacher, Justin, was assigned the job from hell, the position that had to be sold to a newcomer as the job from heaven. He would take on four classes of lower-level students who, the entire first semester, had been taught not by one instructor but by successive substitute teachers. (The district had failed to fill the position permanently in the fall, and the students—mostly struggling readers and members of what the discipline office called the "All Stars," in trouble on a daily basis—had been paying the price.) I walked into the English office one afternoon following Christmas break and found Justin seated at the table, listening as the department chair *yahdah-yahdahed* his assignment and flipped through initial paperwork.

"Our kids are basically good," I overheard her telling him as my back was turned. "They'll be nice classes."

"Great," Justin said, briefly lifting tight fingertips from his forehead.

I slipped out, mumbling something inaudible about how the kids wouldn't be nice at all.

Examples, IV

In the mid-1970s, my family spends five years stationed with my father in Minot, North Dakota, and my mother makes a home for us on my father's military salary. Her "place" seems to be anywhere. Within weeks of our arrival, she appears on the front page of the local newspaper, standing behind a microphone at a city council meeting. Soon after, a stranger calls, a school board member known for her unabashed evangelicalism, big flowery hats, and surgeon husband — a woman who will become a dear friend. "I want you to run for office, Lady," she tells my mother. "What do you say about that?"

Mother runs for city council, then for school board. We sit for brochure photographs in the living room: my mom with a fresh perm, Dad standing in his blue uniform, me with big glasses and a ruffled crêpe blouse, my darling toddler sister. Local town figures visit our kitchen, make the phone ring. One of my mom's supporters, burly and buckskin-jacketed, brags about lugging his television into the backyard and blasting Dan Rather's face from the screen with a shotgun. Mother tells me a group of men show up one night, intimating that more money will flow her way if she agrees to certain positions in advance. "It's how we do things around here, that kind of thing," they say.

She doesn't win either seat, but she becomes part of a local crusade to raise awareness about secular humanism. By age nine or ten, I know all about the Back to Basics movement, Mel and Norma Gabler, the E.R.A., and Phyllis Schlafly. I know the red flags of "moral relativism" in history books and literature. My sister and I color and play with dolls on the marble floors of the state legislature building as Mother and her friend meet with representatives behind a heavy closed door, talking books: The Pigman, The Medium is the Message, Future Shock.

Parties at our house those years run long into the night, and I sneak from my room to the first landing of the white-railed staircase, work my toes into the grey carpet, and try to overhear some coherence in the adult world with its cigarettes and cocktail punch and arguing. The world I long to join.

Each day, from my classroom in a corner of the hallway, I watched Justin pass from one room to the next, jaw forcibly clenched, feet heavy, or awkwardly rushing, briefcase in hand and shoving a lopsided cart loaded with purple textbooks. He looked miserable, as if in this job he'd pledged himself to a girl he'd never been allowed to meet beforehand, a girl I'd known for seven years.

I found something tender in Justin's raw earnestness, his indignation and shock at the daily job. For some colleagues, his struggles were an unwelcome reminder of the isolation in our work and seemed to lay bare how the school as a structure could be brutally unsupportive.

After witnessing one class where a few students shoved books out the crack in a small window, Justin's advisor said there was only one choice, one example to follow: "Do what I do," he said, fierce with alpha male bravado. "I'd pull each of those guys outside and point at their chests and say, 'Stop Being an Asshole.' I'm not afraid to say Asshole."

Justin found this approach useless. In the thick of teaching, the lack of affirmation took a physical toll on Justin's nerves, and he jetted off in the car during lunch for smokes on the patio of his nearby rental house. A few of us gathered him in after work, to rally, joke, and complain at coffee shops, or out for beer and fries. After some weeks, it was mostly him and me. Before we ever spent the night together, we spent hours at the card table beside my kitchen window, playing gin rummy until almost dawn.

Abruptly, there was a handwritten letter on the mat outside my apartment door, the last (and first) I ever received from the man to whom I'd been attached seven years. I had been avoiding his phone calls, and his words now stopped just short of proposing marriage. He was finally ready, he said, to "step up to the plate." He barraged me with calls at school. He planned to find medical treatment for his obsessive compulsive disorder, finish his college degree, start taking pictures again. He wanted to meet somewhere, talk it over. I felt like laughing, because I wanted him to thrive, but not with me.

Why had I acted married all these years—not to a bad man, but a bad match? Perhaps, actually, too much a *match*, not enough challenge to my strengths and weaknesses?

On Mother's Day in a restaurant, days after these changes shook out, I told my mother across a table of eggs and coffee cake. "I'm not with Dan anymore," I said. "I've ended it. Finally. I'm seeing someone new. A good guy."

My mother braced the pink napkin over her mouth. "I knew something was different," she said. And then she was laughing and silly half-crying, pretend-collapsing over her purse in the booth, like a young woman surprised by flowers from someone she thought would never send them.

Examples, V

When I am still a high school student, my dad hands me a thick paperback copy of journalist Edward R. Murrow's biography. I read some of it. He pays me five hundred dollars that summer so that instead of taking my usual law office job, I can "do some writing every day." My dad repeats over and over that I need to be self-sufficient, economically solvent, able to speak up for myself, make money.

One Sunday at a hotel brunch, a few years before he will leave us, I tell my dad that earrings don't necessarily mean a man is gay. Also that not all feminists hate men. My father won't have any of it. "Yes, they are gay," he says. "Yes, they do hate men."

Dad grows silent and I look at my mother, whose hands I can't see under the edge of the table. She tilts her head towards me as he hitches his wallet from a hip pocket.

"Well, yes," she says. "Most of them do, you know."

To this day, in some moments when I'm most discouraged, doubting my right to speak up, it's not my father's frown that comes to mind it's my mother's — blankness in her face above a tight, thin line.

In that seventh spring, I decided to take a temporary unpaid leave the following year, and as colleagues discovered my intentions, I found myself on the receiving end of unsolicited monologues and commentaries. These would be offered abruptly, in line at the copy machine or, confessional-like, across the barrier of bathroom stalls. Voices proclaimed how much they loved teaching, needed to pay their mortgages, cared too much about their own families to change professions. My choice seemed to imply an indictment or demand a defense of their own careers. Who did I think I was?

Life moved forward as the school year came to a close. The first time I stayed at Justin's, he pulled open an empty drawer in the bureau. "Here," he said. "I cleared it out for you." It was something I had taught myself — in the classroom, in my private life — never to expect. I recognized the small, unlikely gesture, its offhand thoughtfulness, by pure contrast: Here was the negative example that felt good.

One night, we watched *High Fidelity*. In the second shot, a closeup of John Cusack's face, I felt something like relief. He was a grownup with pasty cheeks, disappointed and complicit eyes slung low, a frankly jagged bottom row of smoker's teeth. "What came first," he asked into the camera, "the music or the misery?"

"Yeah," whispered Justin. "The misery or the teaching?" A question no one was supposed to ask out loud.

Years later, a professor in a teacher training program will tell me how new candidates come to her with awful stories. "I don't tell them the truth," she will say, shaking her head and looking away from me. "That it will be much worse, much more from left field, later." She will shrug. "Would they become teachers if I described reality?"

Why was it that, when my own life outside the classroom became more satisfying and engaged, school felt less like the right place to be? Was this a failure of my own character, my capacity to commit and endure? Or was something missing from the original engagement? I wondered whether all the strain in the name of students might have always been a kind of camouflage for pains not healed in myself.

The day of end-of-year check-out, I made the annual ritual visit to the principal's office. "You know who you should talk to?" he asked, scratching his name in pen along a faint line at the bottom of the yellow sheet. He shared the name of a teacher who had tried her hand at private security service for a year but then returned to her position at the school. I couldn't tell whether he saw her as an example of failure or success, this woman who now openly lived with him and had her own history of struggling with marriage, several times over.

"Sure," I said. "Thanks."

The principal pushed the paper across his desk and looked at me skeptically, as if I were a pretentious and overpriced sculpture and he didn't get the point. I couldn't blame him. "I've never seen you teach," he said, as I signed my name. "But I hear you do a good job." He offered his big hand awkwardly, the one with the gold watch and wrist bracelet, and I shook it.

Examples, VI

The summer of that seventh year, Justin and I drive from southern California to Connecticut in the dinky convertible he has borrowed all this time from his dad. I am running out of money, with no idea how I will support myself when we return, when Justin leaves for a stint in the Peace Corps. But never does life feel so big as during those days when the cramped car seems open to every disaster and change in our path. On the way to meet Justin's family out east, we encounter the greening scar of Mount Saint Helen's crater, newly-charred forests at Yellowstone, Idaho's lava-pocked Craters of the Moon, the blank space once held by Oklahoma City's Federal Building, a stubble of Anasazi ruins.

Have I become a bad and wasteful person? A teacher losing her mind? At some point, I stop calling home to update my mother, to say hello or check on my cats or mail. All my checks had been post-dated in advance, paperclipped to bill stubs and envelopes, with stamps. I had been so ready.

How do I say I have long dreamed of leaving, driving miles without casting a look back across the rounded slope of my shoulder? Why doesn't it bother me when my mother calls and reports — her voice seeming mostly anxious that I am not anxious — how a cluster of palm trees near my bungalow caught fire one scorching afternoon, and thankfully the fire department came to hose the flames, so my little rooms were safe and sound?

We return to California, a few weeks before Justin will board a plane. The Peace Corps will send him to teach in Ukraine, where native instructors are sometimes paid in sacks of sugar, rice, or flour. At the small airport, I watch him take his place in line on the tarmac, edging closer to the plane, a wool backpack slung awkwardly over his battered leather jacket.

Touching the smudged window between us, I can't tell what feels like the most real thing. He has asked about leaving repeatedly: Should he do it? Should he forget the Peace Corps and stay in California and go to grad school?

All I have is Yes, Yes.

Within days of Justin's departure, I snapped up a temp job at a printing plant, a job that contradicted all the lessons of seven years in a classroom. I enjoyed having an empty car trunk. No more boxes of spiral bound notebooks from students, folders stuffed with copies and jammed in Kinko's bags, forgotten binders from staff training sessions. No loose pens, markers, pencils, no random paraphernalia from class projects. I worked with adults only. I had no salary. Without sick leave or vacation time, I eked by on $12 per hour, clearing about $10, without medical benefits. I paid some bills on credit. I took zero work home and did not spend evenings preparing for the next day of work. If I was sick, I didn't have to work two hours ahead of time, scripting the day for a replacement, trying to anticipate all consequences of my absence. At lunch, a full hour proceeded without interruptions, rather than the half-hour I had grown used to, so often reduced to a handful of minutes, parent calls, tutoring, and a bathroom break. I could read *Crime and Punishment* to the lull of the printing machines, or else I sat at the long, 1970s-style laminate table in the break room and wrote to Justin.

I didn't miss my classroom, and I didn't feel that I had "lost" my way. I loved the frank productiveness of printing, the eye-burning smell of ink from the factory floor that adjoined the offices where I spent most of my time. In isolated moments, I caught glimpses of men standing and cursing inside jaws of the shiplike Heidelberg web machine. They replaced ink tanks and rubber belts, tweaked steel knobs. Threaded two and three ton paper spools into the machine. After the buzzer-bell and the red light alert, the slow then sudden chug sound, the *washa-washa* that echoed everywhere as glossy pages appeared, like gold from straw or occasionally smudged or mis-fed mistakes. I liked how trade printers didn't discriminate, much. Thick, resin-glossed cheerleader catalogues. Democrat and Republican candidate posters and brochures slathered equally in red-white-and-blue. Golf score cards shiny green. PlayBill programs for New York and Los Angeles. Brochures for Seventh Day Adventist "Revelation Seminars." Soft porn on cheap newsprint.

The total product output was so high that no individual project mattered too heavily. My workmates seemed to thank me no matter how tiny the task accomplished. (Perhaps I only noticed this because I had grown used to not being thanked for doing so much more.) "You really saved my ass on that one!" the sales manager might say after I had fixed embarrassing typos in the salutation of a business letter.

People argued or stormed out of meetings but then smoothed things over. For all the class divisions among factory floor workers, the managers, the graphic designers, salespeople, and office support, no one seemed to be claiming that such divisions didn't exist, or that trade printing was some sublime occupation. Frustrations were task or personality related, and not endured as perceived failure of magic or alchemy.

Unlike the school, the factory didn't fantasize about itself. (Ironically, the "factory school," with its programmed curriculum and row desks lacked this factory ethos.) I didn't have to marry the job or pretend that I wanted to marry it. For a while, it was all an incredible relief from the idea that every moment of my profession had to matter.

Another truth, however, became too literal to ignore. The plant manager complained to me one afternoon, breaking from his usual dirty joke tone to face me at the switchboard. "Everything we make — every piece of it — goes from the coffee table to the trash," he said. He leaned his head against the doorjamb. He was right. Ultimately, the disposability was too much.

On my final day, the little desk I'd used was cluttered by handwritten thank-you cards, a gift basket, a Mylar balloon, leftover tiramisu from a farewell luncheon. Nothing like the cryptic silence of stepping away from the classroom.

Surely I could manage again, returning without relying on the misery? I'd learned enough to be a good teacher in the grey areas, somewhere between polar examples, avoiding overdrive. I'd taken a breather. Salary and benefits would offset some of the senselessness and drudgery. I was, after all, fairly good with students. Besides that, Justin and I had each performed enough penitential separation to claim something happy for ourselves, and a temp job didn't seem to fit our plans. He was leaving Ukraine early. We were going to be married.

Examples, VII

One night, I dream: a giant artificial lagoon, surrounded by women and girls. I'm wearing jeans, leather boots, and sit like everyone else right at the cold cement edge. A woman stands where a diving board might be. She seems far away, pronouncing directions as if through a megaphone, without a megaphone. The green water holds itself still, like a slate we might write words upon. In my head, I know the rules better than anyone, so I barely listen. It's as if I have heard the woman in advance. Suddenly: I see the side of a foot, my own foot, drag across the water as if it's not attached to me — boot, pants, leg soaked up to calf muscle. I notice eyes gawking my direction.

"Get out," says the woman. But I am already moving when she speaks. Some faces stare, others gaze down into their hands, at the water, at their own feet. I feel the separation as I make myself stand up. The water wavers a pulse where my boot had been, thrumming away from the water's cement rim, now a small space I've left blank. A space that's closing.

In Greek, the word "pupil" refers not only to the anatomy of the eyeball, and to students, but also means "little doll." In returning to the school I knew so well, to a new cohort of pupils, I returned also to the doll house from which I'd slipped. Professionally, I was the negative example: I had not successfully stayed out of teaching, and I had not sustained my position without leaving it. I re-entered the school somewhat chastened, as a straying wife might return to spouse and children, as a mistress or wayward woman retreats to the nunnery for reform.

I would be paid well. I was going to enter what I hoped was my own healthy marriage outside school walls. But in a nervous tension that tugged between my throat and stomach, my body quickly registered the return as a mistake. Like those seven years with the man I didn't leave, teaching was perhaps still too good a match for my dependencies—my need to look virtuous, dedicated. I tried to push this vague confusion away. I was vetted like a novice with penances to remind me that I must be grateful to be allowed back: assigned extra after-school committee duties, traveling three rooms during the day rather than returning to a single classroom home of my own. No one really spoke to me about leaving, or about coming back. I was marked by my absence and by the concession of my return. (An invisible Scarlet "F"—for Failure? Flight? Floozy?) In some measure, return felt like resignation already.

In American Literature classes that September, my eighth year at a place where I had become a new stranger, we began with John Winthrop's idea of the early colonies as "a city on a hill." This was the positive example all those early founders thought Americans should aspire to be for their God, for the world they believed would scrutinize them. We read essays on commercialism, studied advertisements in magazines and nightly news. We discussed how American aspirations to be perfect had changed, had stayed the same—had created promises we didn't, and couldn't, always keep.

Meanwhile, back in my little bungalow, Justin and I laid out pages of readings from the Bible for our wedding ceremony. Chose our vows.

School was not the promised land, and no one could exactly blame or expel me for tasting the forbidden fruit outside the boundaries. But school was the land of promise, more literally of promises, I had made to myself, for better and worse. In those first seven years, teaching had been like a strange early marriage, arranged if not destined by long-held beliefs that I deserved neither pleasure nor reciprocity. And yet how could I aspire to other promises, model choices now born not merely from discipline, but from passionate embraces? In the classroom, I faced a perpetually filling, perpetually emptying nest. Would I teach as if "being good" in and of itself was good enough for me, enough for my students?

In the last scene of Heinrich Ibsen's *A Doll's House,* Nora stands with her bags at the household door, preparing her husband for an exit that will remove her from the family to whom she has been loyal and devoted for many years. Her husband can't accept this declaration, can't come to see that she is not his doll any longer. Yet in one poignant question, Nora challenges him: "And I—how have I prepared myself to educate the children?" He has no answer. He may not know what she means. In his own mind, he may imagine a group of psychiatrists gathered in a green sitting room to prove Nora's silliness and self-absorption, her cruelty and irrational dissatisfaction. He must be convinced that any other woman in her position would be, in a word, *satisfied.* After seven years, I had finally posed Nora's question to myself, only to discover a braid of uneasy answers raveling and unraveling before me.

Appreciation Day

As an experienced teacher, you will know which of the following statements are completely true and which are only partly true. The exercise in discernment will serve as a team-building test for staff development.

For the week of May 9 through 13, you will find the faculty work-room demarcated for meditation only. Each of you is urged to be present for relaxation at least one twenty-minute lunch period or one full half hour before the first bell each day. Names must be logged in on the time sheet posted near the door.

During this week, copy machines (if not still broken) will not be running, thus reducing noise. The workroom phone will also be disconnected. Please make parent or personal calls and schedule collegial and parent-student conferences during the hours of 3 to 6 p.m. on school premises, or at home per usual. No grading student tests, computer work, or other tasks will be permitted in our staff workroom while we use it as a sacred meditation zone.

Please note: the lights must be kept off at all times. Administration has secured special permission for lighting and burning votive candles during this week, and a volunteer will check and change votives as they burn out. Also, votive holders will need to be cleaned of soot each day, to decrease air toxicity. We have selected the following candle scents, one for each day of meditation week: Home Sweet Cinnamon, Shampoo Buttercream, Rainbow, Minestrone Comfort, and Ocean Children.

Meditation card packets have been placed in your mailboxes as a gift from administration to be employed during meditation time. Teachers are cautioned that they must not bring any articles that can be identified as overtly religious (Bibles, rosaries, statuary, prayer mats, etc.). The VCR/television will run Pilates and yoga tapes throughout the day. No other movies or programming will be permitted, except Oprah reruns for staff granted permission to meditate after school (please apply in office ahead of time). Meditation cards may not be used for poker or other games.

In keeping with our trust and vulnerability theme this year, shoes must be removed and set aside as you enter the room. Teachers will find oils and lotions, towels and manual massage devices laid out on tables against the wall. Electric massagers will be accompanied by orange extension cords courtesy of the district physical plant. These cords and devices may not be taken to classrooms at any time. Meditation mats are already laid out on the floor, covering marks and tears that have been noted on recent work orders.

All relaxation implements must be wiped down with paper towels and returned to the places from which they were borrowed. Cross-gender massage is discouraged, but waiver forms are available in the office. "O" magazines must be returned to the stack.

Cafeteria staff will keep workroom tables stocked with lowfat muffins and grapes. No lunch or breakfast may be brought in from outside. The microwave can be used for low-carb popcorn only. Although some faculty have complained in the past about problems with the coffee maker, hot water will be kept on the burner for making tea. Teabags will not be provided and staff is urged to bring herbal teabags only. Please leave all caffeinated beverages outside the meditation center.

We are happy to offer this meditation reward in appreciation following the April visit from the Western Association of Schools and Colleges (WASC) team. Be aware that your second phase of reports is still due Friday, without exceptions. Meditation logs will be filed as part of our WASC evidence.

It's a happy coincidence that Mother's Day falls this Sunday. This time is yours to celebrate. Regardless of the manner in which you choose to relax, this week and always, your silence means the world to us.

Teacher Training 9-11

The last three years have brought tests we did not ask for.
— George W. Bush, *State of the Nation Address 1/20/04*

*All you have to do, I tell myself, is keep your mouth shut
and look stupid. It shouldn't be that hard.*
— Margaret Atwood , *The Handmaid's Tale*

Before school on September 11, 2001, bad AM radio in my car in the parking lot blares what everyone else is hearing or has already heard: The World Trade Center towers. They're down. Oh my God. It's confirmed.

There's a stunned, quiet quality to the morning as faculty pass each other outside buildings and in corridors, whisper or turn away shaking our heads. There's latent, disturbing excitement as well: Will something else happen? Will a building, a bomb, a plane explode somewhere in L.A.? During the morning's first class, one of my freshmen bursts in wearing a red, white, and blue tank top (perhaps selected as her mother listened to the news?). She whoops, arms held up over her head, cheerleader style: "Yeah! *U – S – A!*"

"Stop," I say as she flops into her desk. "It's not a football game."

I can't exactly blame her for not knowing how to show she takes the tragedy seriously. Many students seem extra watchful for cues from us, yet this sad and scary morning, no direction is forthcoming from the central administration, from any unified body of adults. It occurs to me how, almost twenty years earlier, I had been scratching notes in Government class when our principal's voice came across the intercom to briefly acknowledge the explosion of the space shuttle Challenger. Today there are no sober announcements, no moments of silence. All of us seem wandering as if expecting a divine, or at least official, voice to name the moment. By the next day, someone suggests we assemble students to recite the Pledge of Allegiance outside, under the campus flag. Everyone is encouraged to wear red, white, and blue to show unity. I suggest black. Some of us do wear black.

Another student pulls me aside: "Nobody even knows the national anthem anymore. Suddenly they want us to learn that too?"

Within just a few days, a pre-scheduled curriculum training session for English teachers takes place without disruption. Our patriotic duty? The timing, location, and content of the training session itself enact a strange violence, suggesting a subtext of political and militaristic hype. Does this bother me more, do I notice it, because I've spent a year working outside the school in a print factory?

Our workshop leader starts the morning laying a transparency on the overhead projector: *To maximize the learning of each and every student, we must not get sidetracked by hurdles*. She reads the message to us twice. "This is our charge," she tells us. She means "obligation" or "duty," but I imagine cavalry in movies shouting the same word as they thunder down a hill, think of how we Americans flash plastic to "charge" what we can't afford. She mentioned earlier how she is glad that we're going forward even after the terrorist plane crashes. I suppose we could say we are charging forward.

She clacks fingernails against each other, on the surface of the projector machine. "I looked up the definition of standard," she says, as if the term is new to us. She slips the OED definition onto the projector. The text defines "standard" as a warlike banner people raise and rally around. Tanks and troops come to mind. Brand-name loyalty. People brandishing flag colors football-game style just days ago, after the WTC crumbled in a pulverized heap. "The important part—" our leader says, " —It's a whole lot easier to hit a target standing still." She doesn't mention how hitting a target usually destroys it.

I think of a student the previous day, a boy who told me about his project on bulletproof vests for history class, how he needed a trip to the military surplus store for samples. The same student had been blamed a few years earlier for allegedly threatening to plant bombs on our campus. As I look at the leader's fingernails, magnified ten times on the wall behind her, I want to understand the impulse towards destruction. What it would be like to wear a vest — or carry a weapon?

I'd seen a truck on my way to the training meeting, double-barreled flags flanking each fender, a hand-painted flag across the back window above words in white: *Fear This.*

Our geographical location this morning is Kafka-esque. We've assembled at the District "Nutrition" Center, lodged at a dead end on the west crust of our city proper, near the shriveled Santa Ana riverbed. Three notable landmarks stand nearby: the dog pound; a cluster of silos, each labeled "hydrated lime"; and the camouflage-painted Army surplus store. We can hear the dogs through an open door as the leader proceeds with more mantras, undisturbed by the yelping.

By mid-morning, a second presenter takes the center aisle. "My hat goes off to you, what each of you accomplishes in the classroom," she says. People feign attention, faze in and out. On the projector, the new presenter plants a colorful logo, a circle with the word again, *Standards*, tipped across the middle. She splays her hand over the logo as if she, too, must protect us from the shock of a word we've never seen before.

"So much of what you do is holding down the fort." She sighs for effect. "But this is a really different worldview, a real shift." Her shadowed palm seems clawlike on the wall. "It's really about *living it,* about practicing all the time, marshaling the strategies. We have a cohort document. It's a graph…"

"Fort" and "marshaling," "cohorts" and "strategies." Schools as sites. Test sites. Graph coordinates, targeting. The presenter smiles mildly, eyes wincing that she understands us. I look at the other faces in the room, want to ask my colleagues: *How long have they talked to us this way?*

Like everyone else, I say nothing. Teachers shuffle papers and folders, brows raised, glazed, pretend-listening. We sit in purple chairs at long, gray tables, water bottles and Styrofoam cups empty. The faint smell of baking cookies or bread drifts in from the industrial kitchen. Someone at my table grades essays. Someone else smiles—polite, eager to make the best of it. Another person whisper-jokes about *Soylent Green.*

In the back row, a woman jangles her charm bracelet in the air, asks: "Will all these standards be put together? I mean, side-by-side—like a Bible for all of us?"

Before the presenter can answer, a banging begins in the car lot beyond the window. Presenter Number Two nods Yes to the Bible, to the side-by-side-standards-for-all-of-us. The banging echoes above the sound of yelping dogs. I imagine someone faceless and mute bouncing a giant plastic trashcan.

The presenter points to a yellow flyer now distributed among us—a sheet we've already seen at another meeting on a different color paper, a sheet listing three topics about reading. She recites the text: *Read to your students; read with your students; get them to read on their own.*

"This is the latest," she says.

I scratch the head off a pimple near my hairline and pray I don't bleed. The bangs outside now seem subtly metallic. A vent kicks on and the coffee maker suddenly hisses dragon-like behind us on a back table. A motor growls somewhere outside, muffled and tight, and I can't imagine that it is grass being mowed in this valley of grit and sand and animal liquefaction.

I remember the flash of the morning truck and its flags: *Fear This.*

The first workshop leader interrupts the presentation I've been ignoring. Her voice carries from wherever she's hiding. "Yesterday, at another training session—and I'm not kidding you," she says, "we had a woman literally laid out on the floor at a meeting. And I thought, 'My lands, we *are* killing them.'"

Our laughter, high and sudden, only half-recognizing itself, crushes into the room as if from somewhere else.

Course Contents

We stood in a cluster, on the steps outside the library. We didn't know what to say to one another... We looked at one another's faces and saw dismay, a certain shame, as if we'd been caught doing something we shouldn't.
It's outrageous, one woman said, but without belief.
What was it about this that made us feel we deserved it?
— Margaret Atwood, *The Handmaid's Tale*

I can see the cinder block walls of my classroom painted dingy cream, the shiny white boards with black marks — letters, phrases, numbers, drawings. *These are the standards for today's lesson. These are the Expected Schoolwide Learning Results.* There are the faces of students looking at me, gaping at each other, hungry faces and faces that appear puffy or overfed. Eyes that seem to hide, that say, "I am trying to starve myself." Young bodies and elbows hover over notebooks, over spiral sheets torn at the corner, over open and closed books. Students shake their heads, glare at me, try not to look up from their blank papers. I have read the signals that say they want to tell me everything and nothing, that they will pretend and blather and be silent.

Now I am the department chair. Nothing has changed.

Some days, it seems we are all part human, part machine — what science fiction calls the Borg or cyborg entity, a fusion of flesh with bureaucracy. It is difficult in this terrain to discern any difference.

Cut to: Desks in rows. Eighteen teachers seated in various postures of discomfort, some with arms folded, fiddling with buttons or sweater hem or teasing loose threads on a cuff. Some with legs stuck out straight beyond the metal frame of a desk or into the aisle. One person appears not to listen, works her pen across a three-inch stack of papers. Others peer back over their shoulders, reach for their own stashes of work stowed nearby in bags. Someone complains. Two people whisper and giggle—a dirty joke. Across the room, hands pass a microwave popcorn bag with a black burn mark on the bottom. Hands dig inside. The popcorn rustles. Kernels spill on the floor, lie there. Someone pops an empty plastic bottle against a knee. The agenda seems to have disappeared, but voices without bodies still compose themselves in strange bonds and patterns. "When will they tell us what to do?" "Forget that. What's the point anyway?"

There are stapled packets and loose sheets to hand out: yellow sheets, pink and white sheets, lime green. Typed instructional strategies chunked into paragraphs, massive data tables of student test results, test schedules in three-point font, long district mandates. Sometimes the principal comes in, arms crossed over his barrel chest, and passes out more packets. He wears a charcoal suit and black alligator shoes. His heels clack the tile floor.

"I want you to use these things," he says, looking down at the people seated or squirming in front of him. "Refer to them. I don't want to hear that you're not using these materials."

He's gone, suddenly, the industrial door making a clipping sound as he exits. We are silent, reading.

Vision Statement[1]
We envision a school in which the
professional learning community
demonstrates a culture of shared leadership
that focuses on student achievement.
Students and teachers work together to
articulate individual goals in relation
to grade level standards. Parents receive
clear and on-going communication regarding
their children's progress towards these
goals. We envision a school in which
curriculum is engaging, standards-based,
and goal oriented. Teachers utilize the
most effective researched [sic] based

methods to meet the needs of a diverse
group for [sic] learners.

Using this Workbook: Language and Sentence
Skills Practice[2]
"Choices" worksheets offer up to ten
activities that provide new ways of
approaching grammar, usage, and mechanics.
Students can choose and complete one
independent or group activity per
worksheet. "Choices" activities stimulate
learning through research, creative
writing, nonfiction writing, discussion,
drama, art, games, interviews, music,
cross-curricular activities, technology,
and other kinds of projects, including some
designed entirely by students.

I find myself stepping outside moments as they pass, watching how I listen, eyes wide, my mouth covered with both hands. Sometimes I draw a cornucopia with too many grapes, or an eye floating in the margin of my agenda sheet. Our mumbles pile together like laundry on the floor.

No matter how much time passes, remembering these meetings still embarrasses me. The same questions always lurk underneath the noise: *What does it mean to teach writing and reading – to model listening and speech? What does it mean to be a teacher at all?*

Everyone has a theory. I attend a talk at an independent bookstore near the beach. Teachers, parents, and politicians fill up the foldout seats. The speaker, a writer-teacher I know, offers her advice. "You have to teach who you are," she says. I have heard her repeat this phrase in books and interviews and, on this occasion, tucked behind the bookshelves, someone asks her something about testing, about the straightjacket of standardization. She clutches (wrings?) political T-shirts in her hands as she talks. One depicts stick figures of boys and girls joined together like paper dolls. "Teach who you are," she repeats. I find myself nodding along with the heads in the rows in front of me.

Yet, any given moment, I have not been so sure who my "I" is, exactly, or what special business that "I" has had to teach anyone. Rare moments of certainty have only come, I think, from the unwieldy knowledge that I am not a Stepford being, not a unitary entity who pulls the string, presses "play" and "record," moves her mouth over a tray of Rice Krispies treats, a PowerPoint presentation, a worksheet.

Use of District Pacing Charts[3]
[...] All subject-alike teachers in all
departments are to work collaboratively to
ensure that their instruction is aligned
with the approved pacing charts, district
standards and assessments and that all
students are being successful. For example,
all Introduction to English teachers'
instruction should be in approximately the
same place on the pacing chart at any given
time in the school year. [...]

Tim, a student in a remedial class, delivers an informational talk on Mario Lemieux, the Pittsburgh hockey star whose image has been tacked to the front of my room since the first day of school. Tim barely looks down at the single notecard in his hand while he rattles off goals, assists, and team statistics, but what really gets to me is his visual aid. Using merely a pencil, he has sketched out a giant close-up of Lemieux's face. Tim has transposed these giant dimensions from a 3"x 3" sports photo, which he props on the chalk tray next to the poster while he talks. Because I have seen him drawing in class, I know that he likes to draw, so I believe that he made the poster himself. I scratch notes on his score sheet and he earns a "C+" for the speech. He wants me to keep the poster. *Yeah. Kissing up,* say some of his classmates. When he hands the poster to me, I see a slight crease and smudge in an upper corner where he had tried not to bend it, bringing it to class. *Thanks, Tim,* I say.

I fit the drawing in an old frame and hang it on a wall behind my desk at home. When my husband and I move from our newlywed apartment to our small, half-timber house, we hang the drawing in the kitchen, near the coffee machine and the phone.

The posterboard washes out against the frame's white paint, so that Lemieux's pencil outline seems like a shadow above Tim's signature.

Implementation of English Language Arts
(ELA) materials[4]
When reviewing your artifacts, I did not
see definitive data that the majority of
your teachers were integrating the new
materials into their instructional program.
These are questions that I have: 1) how did
the teachers use the entry level diagnostic
data? 2) where are the minutes from their
department meetings that demonstrate
collaboration on units of study, use of
pacing [charts] and common assessments?
3) I did not see any interventions listed
for ELA students at risk of failure and
4) there was no data submitted regarding
student achievement in ELA.

Six long tables fit together to shape a boardroom table. I am a guest here, listening. A famous university compositionist stands at the narrow end of the table. She tells her grad students about a memo she's presenting to a committee, a formal demand for smaller class sizes in the university writing program: twenty students to one teacher—"the maximum," she says. I can picture her words in tight black font across the bonded paper, her signature in fine black calligraphy at the bottom of the page. She stands now, a presence like a giant period at the head of the classroom, and says that no one can teach writing on a larger scale. (In a previous class session, she has admitted that the little she knows about primary and secondary school workloads comes to her through friends).

I picture a telegraph service, clicking and beeping bulletins on ticker tape: CALIFORNIA K THRU 6 INSTRUCTORS WORK WITH AN AVERAGE OF 33 STUDENTS FOR 6 SUSTAINED HOURS AT A TIME STOP CALIFORNIA 7 THRU 12 INSTRUCTORS WORK WITH AN AVERAGE OF 36 DIFFERENT STUDENTS EACH HOUR FOR 5 CONSECUTIVE HOURS DAILY STOP A PUBLIC SCHOOL TEACHER OF ENGLISH COMPOSITION IN CALIFORNIA COULD WORK WITH UP TO 180 STUDENTS A DAY STOP SINCERELY YOUR FRIENDS

Giving Student Feedback/Managing the Paper Load[5]
Not everything that a student writes must be grades [sic], or even read, in order to have an effect on the student's skill development.

How Can I Evaluate a Stack of Papers Quickly?[6]
Try a "positive comment sheet." Type a list of positive comments and key them to a number code. On the student's paper, write the letters which correspond to the comment you wish to make.

Instructional Procedures for Independent, Unassisted Repeated Reading[7]
Direct the student to the practice center or to his or her seat to practice reading the selection while the next student reads to the assistant. You may wish to instruct the student to use a stopwatch and keep records of words read per minute (WPM) for

```
each reading practice. The reading practice
may be done silently, but the testing is
done orally.
```

Abby sits in front. She raises her hand. She argues in that friendly way that gets other classmates to contribute more openly. She lets her voice get loud. She struggles with essays, sentence by sentence, asks for approval, for feedback. She shows up to class early. "Getting better, right?" she says. "You'll recommend me for Advanced Placement, right?"

Yes, I will.

She brings flowers sometimes, roses or zinnias with stems wrapped in damp paper towels. She lays these on her desk next to her notebooks. Some mornings, she brings muffins and hot coffee to teachers whose classes she no longer takes. She's a favorite. We love her.

It is already years later. Behind the lectern, I sit on a stool with my hands tucked under my hips. There is a roll sheet in front of me — dot matrix printed names and numbers with bubbles to mark for tardies and absences. I ignore the list, search around the group of student faces, an afternoon class, watching me. I am stuck somewhere dark when I speak up.

"Abby...Moyers?" I say.

The students blink at me, shake their heads slow and blank, listen for more information. The teacher is "out of it" today, maybe. How should they know?

"A student from here," I go on. "Maybe your brothers or sisters knew her?" One of my hands is moving in the air now, adding questions to the questions. I look down at the roll sheet, pick up a pencil. "You know that place where Chicago Avenue curves down the hill?"

"Yes," one student says. Some nod. Two in the back are comparing homework notes.

I'm lost. There's no way to attach the information. I tell them anyway, "She lost control of her car. Last night. She went over the median and down into the ravine."

Using this Study Guide: Approaching the Novel[8]
The successful study of a novel often depends on students' enthusiasm, curiosity, and openness. The ideas in "Introducing the Novel" will help you create such a climate for your class. Background information in "About the Writer" and "About the Novel" can also be used to pique students' interest.

Julia is a ravenous mind. She's already had a play produced at the Little Globe in San Diego by the time she enters my eleventh grade honors class. She's also a gifted artist who works with pen and paper media, does some painting. She crosses her arms when she listens intently, and she can laugh and snarl at the same time. Kids say that she's as deadpan as Daria, the MTV cartoon character with straight hair and big round glasses—except Julia is the Chinese version. The spring she writes her research paper, she's on a Henry Miller binge, and I'm woefully inadequate as a teacher. She hangs around my desk at lunch, drags over a chair. Her forearms plunk down on her knees. She brings out a paper she has written, points to my comments. "Honors students want answers," she begins. She adjusts the glasses on her nose. "It's frustrating when you just say, 'This is interesting,'" she tells me. She snarls, smiling.

Two or three years after she graduates, Julia returns. I am in a different classroom, working with another student after school: another class, another essay. She waits. "I just wanted to... apologize," she says. She's been gone—to college in New York, then to China, teaching English. "Oh my *God*," she says. I see the smile and snarl again. Her glasses are new, sharper looking, with narrower frames and lenses. She seems to be laughing at herself. "My meetings with students... I started thinking about how I acted. *Wow.* I'm just sorry."

I try not to make a big deal out of this. She's not here to ask for a recommendation, or advice, or anything at all. It's rather lovely. We talk about changes at the school, about how the campus lawn has been torn up for renovation. Trees have been dug out. The ground is muddy everywhere except where there's cement.

I give her a ride home. As I pull the car into her neighborhood, I recall that I've been here before. We realize that her parents lived for years across from the house where my best friend in high school lived before she went to Germany. The families know each other.

"Small world," I say. We laugh at the cliché.

The following summer, after my husband and I get married, we receive a postcard in Julia's characteristic scrawl—watch for a package, she says, a Chinese scroll she hired a scribe to transpose especially for us. On the postcard, she includes the translation in English of the traditional Chinese poem. Part of it goes: *The peach tree is slender and sturdy. The girl is ready for marriage.*

One day the scroll arrives in a cardboard tube on our doorstep. We take the composition to Mr. Lee, the best framing artist in town. He unrolls the rice paper and stares down at the black-brushed characters. He looks up at us, as if curious how such a piece of writing came into our hands. "This is excellent skill," he says. "Person knows what he's doing. The letters. Perfect."

We choose a cherry wood frame flecked with gold and a tea-green matte for the rice paper poem. When Mr. Lee has finished, we hang the framed text on a wall adjacent to the fireplace.

I receive a teachers' edition of the new literature anthology, shiny and huge with sharp corners. Not all the ancillary materials have arrived

TEACHER AT POINT BLANK

when the year begins, but many pieces have been distributed: pre-fab quiz guides, answer keys, grammar packets, vocabulary worksheets, study guides—all smooth and stacked and kraft-wrapped together in heavy industrial bundles. One key element missing is a glossy spiral booklet called "On Course: Mapping Instruction," the week-by-week corporate template for a productive English course.

The school librarian emails me that novels are "locked down" per directive from the principal. The librarian has turned away teachers who want to check out copies of *The House on Mango Street* or *Brave New World* or *To Kill a Mockingbird* for their classes. Teachers are emailing me, since I'm now department chair, calling me with questions.

I am standing in the office of my principal. "No more novels," he says. "Except maybe in advanced level classes."

"Who says?" I ask.

The answer is nebulous: something about officials wanting to improve test scores, how the newly published textbooks will do more for students than reading whole pieces of literature. The new books have number and letter codes for standards printed in the margins alongside the logo of a California bear. The new planning maps are supposed to protect teachers from tangents—red print for required tasks, black print for options.

"Why don't we call our classes test prep seminars?" I ask.

He waves his hand. "I know, I know." He lowers himself to the giant leather chair behind his desk and grabs at the padded arms. "But this is the game we're playing now," he says. "This is what you're going to do." On the wall behind him, the familiar framed image of Al Pacino glares at me.

Walking back to my classroom across campus, I remember something odd from my childhood: that jumbo box of crayons with sharpener attached. In coloring books, I used to emphasize the outlines by pressing the waxy point of each crayon hard into the rough-grained paper before I colored in the shapes.

I'm angry that it's still so easy, this instinct to play the good girl.

Important Warning about Plug in Air Fresheners[9]
Plug in air fresheners are prohibited in any district facility. [...] Employees tend to focus their attention on classroom furnishings and building materials as a source of their complaints, rather than easily controlled sources of chemical contamination introduced into the environment by staff members with good intentions. Few consumers equate any potential risk factors with a product appearing as innocent as an artificial air freshener, yet the health risk is real to many individuals.

Dear Parents or Guardians,[10]
As most of you are aware, a student made a threat in an Internet chatroom to come to school with a gun on Friday, May 16th. An anonymous tip was made to the FBI who immediately contacted the local authorities. The student was taken into custody several hours before school started Friday. The Police Department was on campus for most of the day to conduct a full investigation. Because the incident only involved one suspect, who was in custody, there was never a danger to any student on campus. [...]

I take down a giant green volume I store on a shelf in my office—a thousand pages of teacher names in alphabetical order, cross-referenced by states and cities via an index at the end. I have opened the book, *The Who's Who of American Teachers,* only twice before. The copyright pages mark it as almost ten years old. In a preface paragraph, someone anonymously important writes, "As teachers you are leaders...We must dare to think new thoughts."

I grab a hunk of pages open and stare. Each page is arranged in three columns of type. The type is five-point size, maybe smaller. Short biographies after each name are grouped in alpha-numeric codes for degrees and committees, credentials and classes taught. Without my face close to the page, I could be looking at another language. It might as well be Braille to the seeing eye, except there are no raised bumps to touch with fingertips. It could be a death index, but we are supposed to be proud for landing here. Students nominate us. We can pay sixty-five dollars if we want to own a copy of the book and look at ourselves here, stored on a shelf somewhere. I decide not to look for my name.

Before I put the book away, I examine the gold embossing on its cover. The title is accompanied by the registered trademark symbol, an "R" inside a circle. Corny, I think. Overkill. I pick at the little "R" with my fingernails—not a scratch.

Email to Secondary Education Specialist[11]
"Worthwhile" isn't a word I'm hearing
teachers say lately.
What I'm hearing are words and phrases
like "demoralized," "disconnected from
my students," "strangled," "where are the
materials, anyway?", "cornered," and even
"insulted": why have a master's degree in
English if all we need to do is follow some
xerox of a corporate lesson plan? why do
we have to tap dance in order to earn the
"privilege" of teaching novels to "regular"
kids? [...] Jo Scott-Coe

Email to Principal[12]
In regard to Jo's email(s): This is
becoming too personal...I think that it's
interesting that Ms. Scott [sic] still
refers to "teaching novels." Hasn't she
seen the test scores yet? We need to be
focusing on student learning and not just
what's good for "teachers." I don't have
a problem with Ms. Scott [sic] stating
her opinion which she has already done on
several occasions but this is becoming
ridiculous...we need to move on. [Angela,
Director of Secondary Education]

The Press-Enterprise: "Novels' Use in
Schools Clarified"[13] It's all just a
misunderstanding, say officials... [M]iddle
and high school teachers can use novels
to teach literature, district officials
said. The explanation came after word
spread last month that the great works had
been struck from the English curriculum
this school year in favor of an anthology
textbook...."It was never said that they
were forbidden from using novels, just not
required to teach the novels," [Angela]
said.

Michael, the swimmer with big shoulders, the guy who seems to steep in thought before raising his hand to speak up about what we read in class, he's standing at the edge of my desk, then taking a seat and producing two folded pages from behind his back. It's after class, lunchtime. He wants to talk about a piece he's writing, a college entrance practice we've been revising for a few weeks.

I pretend not to be surprised, but notice that I lean my whole body towards the desk, away from him. Michael listens with his eyes. His paragraphs detail a moment of panic, being stuck in a Speedo and puking before a swimming tournament. It's so extreme, I don't know whether to believe that it really happened. I don't ask—well, maybe I jibe a little. "Yeah," he says. "I really want this essay to be good."

From then on, I look forward to seeing him. More than that: I notice him. He attends all the extra credit literary readings I encourage kids to catch at the university, the community college, the arts center. He's usually with a big batch of girls. They look for me and wave across the seats in the crowds. When Michael asks for a college recommendation, I am not only happy to write it—I gush one out. He's amazing. He's an asset. He's creative. He's humble. He chaperones the ladies. He doesn't talk—he just *does* things.

As I hand him the envelope that spring, I am wondering if he'll believe anything I've written. I don't know if I'm imagining or projecting it, but he seems to withdraw into a posture of assessing me. He seems quieter. Because he sits in the very back row, I try teaching from the side of the room when he's there, to stay out of his normal range of vision.

For the rest of the year, I find myself guilty—some mornings even dressing with him in mind, and praying he's gay.

What Reading Does for the Mind[14]
*High school students should read about two million words each year (about 40 minutes each day) in school and about two million (about 40 minutes each night) outside of school.
*The more than two million words should generate the 4,000 words needed to keep up in vocabulary growth.
*Only the top 25% of students read this much. Average students read less than half of what is needed and the bottom 20% read only 8% of what is needed.

The last day of finals, after students have gone, I pick up the phone in my classroom. It's R's mother. "I'm calling about his grade," she says. "He didn't deserve a 'C' on that research paper, you know, but I won't challenge the mark unless he ends up with less than a 'B' in your class."

I stand at my desk, stare at the bulletin boards from which I've stripped the decorative paper, posters, samples of student writing. On one of the boards all year, stenciled letters in yellow paper used to spell out, *How's your integrity today?*

"I'm grading his final tonight," I say. "Quarter and semester totals will be complete by the morning." I reach for my plastic travel mug, which is empty. I put it to my lips as if I believe there's something left. This gesture has become a habit, I realize, because I rarely have time to fill up my mug once I get here in the morning.

"That research paper was confusing, anyway," she continues. "If there's one thing I know, it's *literature*."

"Okay," I say. "I'll call tomorrow." I lay the phone, comma like, in its plastic cradle. My essay exams to grade for the day are packed up in a brown cardboard box. My desk drawers are empty, the desktop bare except for the plastic mug and a three-hole punching device. I already know that R has earned a 'C,' maybe a 'C+'. He's missed assignments. His written exams have been up and down. He hasn't come for help. He never did ask questions about the "confusing" research project. He's been generally passive and snide in classroom discussions with peers. He sneered when I handed him a memoir about his favorite sport, basketball, a book titled *Glory Days*. I remember him tossing it back on my desk after class without saying a word.

Next morning, I call R's mother. "He made it," I say. "Barely."

"That's great," she says. And then, as if we are sharing small talk in a busy line at a coffee house: "So, I hear you're leaving the school?"

ENDNOTES

[1] Taken from packet of handouts at Instructional Council meeting November 4, 2002. The reference to "professional learning community" is part of a new lingo at the time, often reduced to the acronym PLC. Grammatical errors are included as in the original.

[2] Holt, Rinehart and Winston. *Language & Sentence Skills Practice: Support for the Holt Handbook.* 2002-03: x — No copyright date is printed in the text, but teachers received it as part of a supplementary materials package during the above school year.

[3] Assistant Superintendent of Secondary Education, Superintendent's Office. Memo to 7-12 Principals. August 12, 2002: 2-3.

[4] Assistant Superintendent of Secondary Education. Memo to Principal. October 31, 2002 — Each high school principal had been expected to generate "artifacts" and "data" to prove that English teachers were using all new Holt, Rhinehart and Winston materials.

[5] Secondary Literacy Document. May 17, 2004 — Labeled as DRAFT. Distributed for summer school staff development June 11, 2004. Statement attributed to Gene Stanford. Unclear whether typo was part of original statement or occurred in transcription.

[6] Secondary Literacy Document. May 17, 2004 — Labeled as DRAFT. Distributed for summer school staff development June 11, 2004.

[7] California Department of Education. *Strategic Teaching and Learning.* 168.

[8] Holt, Rinehart and Winston. *Study Guide: Nathaniel Hawthorne, The Scarlet Letter with Connections.* 2002-03: 3 — No copyright date is printed in the text, but teachers received it as part of a supplementary materials package in the above school year. HRW publishes such guides for all novels reprinted under their aegis. The Guide resembles *Cliffs* or *SparkNotes* except its physical dimensions are 8.5" x 11".

[9] Risk Management Memo to Principals and Managers in the District. November 1, 2002 — Printed on pink paper.

[10] Principal's letter to school parents. May 19, 2003 — The school community had already heard of the incident over the weekend, via TV and newspaper reports, including one in the *Los Angeles Times.* There was never any specific communication to the full assembly of staff, faculty, or students. Several teachers reported not receiving copies of the parent letter to distribute.

[11] Email to the Secondary Education Specialist. September 5, 2002 — I wrote this email as Chair of the English Department. Not all materials which teachers were required to use had arrived at the school site, and the apparent "prohibition" on use of novels in classes remained unresolved at the time.

[12] Director of Secondary Education. Email to Principal. September 5, 2002 — Principal summoned me to discuss my email and gave me a copy of the response he had received.

[13] Michael Coronado and Marcia T. Garcia. "Novels' Use in Schools Clarified." *The Press-Enterprise.* October 12, 2002: B1, B7.

[14] "What Reading Does for the Mind." Secondary Literacy Document. Draft. April 12, 2004 — Distributed for summer school staff development June 11, 2004. Statistical sources were not documented in the packet.

Don't Touch the Children

Not when they fall to the grimy floor or scruffy asphalt, not when they cry or suddenly tear into each other's hair, shirts, pockets, or folders. Not if they open their arms and ask for a hug. Not when they turn green, show you a bee sting, have a seizure, or cower along the wall. Not when you see them trying to cover up pimply cheekbones, cracked eyeglasses, fat tummy, stained pants.

Don't graze an arm or hand by accident. Remove yourself from the scene if they draw a weapon or brandish a French fry, or if you suspect a water bottle is really filled with vodka. Placing your body in the middle of two or more student bodies fighting, even to protect one or both or all of them, is a no-no. Avoid direct eye contact. Even a handshake or high-five can put you at risk. Don't point or do anything that could be inferred as pointing. Do not touch any property belonging to a student. Do not look at or attempt to inspect any property belonging to a student. Leave this for someone who does not know the student, or for an animal such as a trained drug dog.

As a last resort, use proximity in establishing trust (bend down near face or desk-level) or asserting dominance (stand over anyone seated or shorter than you). Such methods are less likely to provoke lawsuits and much easier to explain to most parents. Never raise your voice. (Schools with microphones are now making progress to eliminate yelling altogether.) Students with sore throats must not be given cough drops or aspirin though you may, at least in California, counsel students regarding personal birth control, pregnancy, or abortion.

Don't be alone with a child unless the door to your room is open, signaling intent not to molest. (The likelihood of being alone with a child in a room crowded with children is rare but may seem tempting as an antidote to chaos.) Do not fall into the trap of one-on-one contact as an opportunity to concentrate or break through. Keep in mind, always, that you could lose your job or, at least, your reputation.

Be aware that these guidelines are not reciprocal. Students will occasionally: touch your hands, smear mud on your slacks, grab your hemline or your hair. They may poke holes in the family pictures you post on the bulletin board, or drop the glass frame you had placed on your desk. They may take food from your desktop, desk drawers, your refrigerator—sometimes because they are starving, and sometimes because they want to be mean. They may look inside your purse, or take it from your desk (this is why you should keep your purse with you at all times, unless you keep a locked cabinet). They will sometimes swarm around your desk, talking all at once. They will interrupt you, and each other. They will talk about your makeup or lack of makeup, the shape of your body, your shoes and how many pairs you do or don't have, the expensiveness or cheapness of your clothes. They will comment on the rip in your tights, the ink on your fingers, your five-o'clock shadow. They will certainly touch each other. They will ask about your teeth and what happened to them. They will pass notes they want you to notice and wonder about. They will write your name on desks and on websites and superimpose your face over photographs. They will demand to meet you in private, demand to be liked, will tease you with secrets. Those who can drive may follow you to the parking lot or follow you home. They will keep coming, will leave with no warning, then pop up again— in the paper products aisle at Vons, at the gas station, in the liquor store.

Other cautions: Don't talk too loud or tell jokes. Don't react spontaneously to any misbehavior or kindness. Don't address private notes of encouragement, reprimands, or questions to students in your own handwriting, which can be used against you in a court of law. Don't express doubts about anything except your own judgment.

Do: say you're sorry whenever you can. Keep in mind that you are not a private citizen. And remember that teaching works best when performed from remote control.

In the Body of Mary Kay

I am like a child here, there are some things
I must not be told. What you don't know
won't hurt you, was all she would say.

— Margaret Atwood, *The Handmaid's Tale*

I know how to bring out the best in people.
To make them understand.
I wish it was me out there fighting for me.

— Mary Kay Letourneau to a friend in 1999,
as quoted by Gregg Olsen in *If Loving You Is Wrong*

July 7: Morning

This journal does not need to be published. At least that's what local workshop leaders assure us, assure all of us here at this one-week, state-sponsored mini-institute for summer writing. They call upon our desire for "privacy" in the journals, for "creative space." Yet we have sworn no oaths to silence, have taken no pledges to secrecy. We should write, they tell us, what we really feel, what we think. We have nothing to fear. No one has forced us to be here. Our activities this week fall under the category of "professional development." But we are writing for ourselves for a change. *Ourselves.* The idea is: we're fried from teaching students and testing them, from telling students how important writing is, from commenting on students' writing (so much assigned and forced). We need a break, we need social time, we need to cultivate our capacity for self-expression. And no one ever needs to know.

Today is the first day and we have assigned seating. Everybody walks into the trailer classroom in the morning to the sounds of classical piano music. Everybody signs in at a table near the doorway, then finds a seat and writes in a journal until they tell us to stop. I arrived a little early, so I have some more time. We can grab pink melon wedges or Danishes from the snack table, fill styrofoam cups or travel mugs with coffee or tea. Today, per public-school-usual, the bottom of the coffeemaker got scorched. After lunch the rhythm will be similar: classical piano, snacks, and adding to our journals. Fifteen minutes for writing each time, which doesn't seem like much for a writing institute. (I must add to these entries later, at home.) Most of our time during workshops and sessions this week will be reserved for talking about activities we can do with students. I wonder: without all the talking about students and lesson plans, would our work here be considered valid or worthy, or real? Something about the possible answers feels vicarious. This bothers me. Can we be committed to writing as much as we must be committed to students?

Just now, a workshop leader wrote across the whiteboard: *What turns you on about learning?* (A question that made me wonder: What turns you on in the classroom?) And then I started thinking about Justin last night, how he came to bed after me and cupped his naked body against mine, let his hand start exploring. I love to teach the morning after that happens, love to hold that secret under my skin.

I realized years ago that being a whole person, a human body, in a classroom was anything but a matter of paper and ink. We are taught to acknowledge the sexuality of our students as a kind of powder keg or tripwire—how many English teachers have taught *Romeo and Juliet* as moralistic evidence of young and beautiful, ultimately destructive, passion? It's strange that the balance seems tipped, rather awkwardly, towards sterilizing ourselves.

But I think teachers have to know their minds and bodies, know their desires, in order to generate energy in classrooms. How can we maintain healthy boundaries unless we acknowledge and respect where our selves end and the students' selves begin? It's odd to me that before women were ever permitted to be students and teachers, the template of seduction was an open question in the education of men. Disgusting as it sounds now, for example, sexual expression, for Plato, was a serious, even grave, phase of the instructional process. But there was an ethical code, too: the good teacher always had an obligation to draw out the student's physical attraction and love to inspire learning, but then the teacher had to detach from that affection so that the student could move on.

We seem to think we're beyond all that now. But maybe we're just pretending the sexuality isn't there, or that it exists only in the Student Body. (Teachers, after all, are "Faculty," like disembodied brainpower or a bundle of nervous functions.) If we don't ignore sex, we can get transfixed by some Van Halen Hot-for-Teacher gaze from students. We may perform a twisted, cartoonish version of the Playmate teacher because it's the most readily available mirror. We turn into objects, not subjects.

Still, the workshop asks: *What turns you on?*

I confess that energy of sex, its discreet mysteries, is actually like a lifeline for my classroom survival—thinking of Justin's touch, say, at the very moment I'm answering a student's question about vocabulary notes or an essay by Emerson, or in the quiet time when I'm sorting papers as students finish writing an exam, allows me to have knowledge of myself as a body. And this doesn't have to be a perverted liability or an exploitative tool: I can translate my affections in a healthy way.

I love sending out pheromones of desire, willing a contagion of erotics underneath the grammar, the reading, the essay assignments, the blasé directions-giving. It's possible to create an intense dreaminess, an awe about the power of words and how people both use words and live inside them. The recognition can be so magical. *What am I in love with?* I wish they'd ask us that.

Justin and I laugh about how, because of our five-year age difference, he technically could have been my student. We actually met as colleagues and ended up getting married. It's not an especially sensational story for a general audience, compared to the daily dose of news about coaches who blatantly talk up the bodies of female students, or the female teachers who become so concerned about aging in front of students that they splurge on boob jobs and liposuction instead of Ph.D.s or even vacations. I've known teachers and administrators fairly open about swinging. Several years ago I attended a study skills conference at a resort also hosting a "lifestyles" conference for partner-swapping. The continuum of behaviors is vast, but some teachers seem deeply susceptible to whatever might shatter the sense that, for many hours during the workday, we can feel like shadows, like ciphers with voices.

Even within our "scrubbed clean" fantasy of the schoolroom, there are strange surprises. I remember one morning my first year teaching, during my conference period, when I looked through a stack of academic magazines in the English teachers' lounge, and found a hardcore porn magazine — animals and dildos, just everything. I couldn't stop gaping for a moment or two, then couldn't get it out of my mind: who stowed this thing in the lounge? I wished so much to be older and crankier, perhaps married, able to whip that thing out during lunch and ask: *So, fellas, ladies: who dropped this one?* But I was a virgin (at least technically), a brand new employee and a former student at the school. It was just too embarrassing. When I checked later, the magazine had vanished. And I had to laugh.

July 7: After lunch

More piano music. The room was empty except for the program leaders and me, but I signed in anyway.

Why am I in such a hurry to come back here? I think of those kids who get in trouble at school — skirmishes, drinking, profanity, little stuff like tardies or the predictable defiance — all because they want to stay at school. They're sick of school but also prefer school to home, school seems safer with adults they both love and dread. They complain but fill their cup to brimming with detentions and Saturday classes. They rarely earn a major suspension or anything that takes them off campus for too long. Maybe some of us teachers are like that, too. Two retirees I know say they substitute these days, not for the money, but for the stimulation. It makes me wonder what kind of shot in the arm I expect in a summer workshop. And what do I want from a writing workshop where our writing doesn't need to matter?

I remember how a fellow teacher reacted when I took my temporary leave three years ago, how she told a colleague that she always figured my heart had never really been in teaching from the beginning. But isn't it possible that being able to teach requires being able to do lots of other things in life, like maybe breathing or writing without thinking about students?

Another teacher at a state function in Sacramento got really mad at me for raising this question. She was about to retire, and she mentioned that she'd once been a musician but hadn't even *tuned* her piano in twenty-five years, so I said something about how sad that was, that our profession somehow made us feel we had to choose. I'll never forget how she just glared at me, kind of horrified, and said, "I *love* my kids. I *love* my job."

It was almost as if she was challenging me: *What good are you as a teacher if you haven't given up what you love most?* I talked to another colleague recently, a good friend who used to write detective stories, who used to share installments of his novels with me. I asked about how that was going lately, and he said that writing was a gone life for him—"Another lifetime," he said. "It's vanity now." I felt sad, but not in a patronizing way because I understood what he meant. Teaching can cost you. But then I felt a little ashamed, too, because as writing teachers we spend a lot of time persuading students to make time for writing. We tell them they should be lifelong readers and writers.

But maybe students sense that we don't mean it—or, at least, that we aren't sure.

July 7: Evening

I need to say that the first "Reader's Study" session in the afternoon today was kind of strange. The professor stood up there with Tim O'Brien's book, *The Things They Carried,* open to its first few pages, and she asked these *who what when where how?* type questions, like we were sixth graders who might not have done the reading. It may seem strange how a group of teachers can revert so easily into kid mode, but it also makes sense because most of our time is spent with non-adults. Nobody raised their hands, which meant that the same three people kept calling out answers. It was a bit painful.

The scene reminded me of a meeting where a district official gushed to me about reading a book by Isabelle Allende. The woman went on and on about how Allende's book followed the mythic hero pattern we teach our kids. I thought: do we only read serious books because we'll need to teach key terms to new readers? Why are we teachers always reading and gushing about the same big books, quoting the same reviews from NPR, talking like we're prepping a lesson? I guess the answer might be that we rarely get the chance to do anything else. Unless we get into a writing workshop, where we can end up acting just like kids.

July 8: Morning

I'm staring at something they call "the Author's Chair." Actually, it's more stool than chair, like a tuffet with a plump round cushion on top. No one has actually sat there yet, but the workshop leaders say it's purely a voluntary thing. There's a beautiful handmade placard on a nearby table, with black calligraphy spelling out "Author's Chair" in a flourish next to a cartoon sketch of a lush armchair. One leader told us that a former student created the placard for her.

The past two days, the stool and sign have just been sitting there at the front looking empty. But at the end of the day, if anyone has any writing they want to read, there's an allotted fifteen minutes where we can sit on the stool, or stand in front of it, and share from our journals.

I confess something bothers me about this. There's no expectation that everyone will read, that they will write anything *worth* reading, and there's certainly not enough time for everyone to get a word in even if we each wrote something great. But I watched other faces when the professor explained how the author's chair worked, and a few of the women who'd attended in past years were nodding and saying how terrific this had been before, what a great experience for everyone, and I could tell that some of them were really looking forward to their own moment. Starved for it. But yesterday, no one read.

July 8: After lunch

Today's morning workshop was all about how to integrate poetry into the curriculum. The goal is getting kids to make their own books. Both presenters kept pointing to numerical codes of state standards to justify how we could justify doing these projects if someone in administration wants a justification.

Speaking of writing, I'm still not getting why we teachers aren't doing more writing during the day. Maybe someone in authority is worried that if we got too interested, or too good at it, we might leave teaching — or, worse, stick around and publish things. It's more likely they know we like to pretend and play at writing because, after all, wouldn't we be writers instead of teachers if we were really serious? Maybe we believe that old adage from Shaw about teaching as something *other than* actually doing something. But authority and authorship are more than just etymologically connected. How long can I stay in a profession where the line has become so brittle between my own writing and the writing I'm supposed to be inspiring (or demanding) from students?

All these daily activities are starting to feel like knitting or a bridge club—something for the tired, nervous, and overworked ladies to do with their time.

July 8: Evening

A woman volunteered to read for the author's chair today, and she ended up crying. She read this piece about an uncle's surgery, and how the family thought he was going to get better, and then he did get better, but his family went into terrible debt because of medical expenses, and thank God they were still surviving. Women were wiping their eyes or covering their foreheads as they listened, and at the end everyone applauded and one of the workshop coordinators asked the woman how she felt and she said, "Better. I feel so much better."

Glad as I was for her (and sorry, too), that response got me wondering again about whether this institute is really about writing so much as it's about private relief, even therapy? This way, if we believe we've achieved a buzz from some vague sense of emotional support by the end of one week, we're satisfied. Or maybe we're settled down, inspired (sedated?) for the summer. Are we lonely teachers looking for therapy, but because we're too proud to call it "therapy," we call it "writing"?

July 9: Morning

Teachers walking ahead of me from the parking lot today were talking about a local scandal several years ago: An English teacher was handcuffed at a nearby middle school and taken away for having sexual contact with female students. He pled guilty and was convicted on thirty-two counts of lewd acts with a child under fourteen years old. Many of the girls he targeted could barely speak English, and some had undocumented family members. He had traveled on a church mission to South America before taking a teaching job, and was married with children of his own.

"He was Mormon," one of the teachers was saying, as if that answered some question. They argued a bit about whether he had been arrested on campus or not, but what interested me most was how this teacher had used his knowledge and authority in two languages to intimidate girls into sexual activity and silence, at least for a time. He had used the girls' limited capacities in English as a powerful weapon, then went to jail.

By the time I was getting signed in, I was thinking about a different case: Mary Kay Letourneau, the woman teacher who slept with a twelve-year-old and had two babies from him and went to jail a few years back. Then married him after her incarceration was over.

Our standards seem so clear, but they're also a bit oversimplified. Just two days ago we had that question on the board about what "turns us on," and we never got around to discussing possible answers. Yet how many times do we glow about "turning on" students, or getting "turned on by" students, even though what we mean is "excited" about books and essays and giving speeches or writing poems? I'm really wondering what "normal" teachers might have in common with the ones who end up transgressing, crossing the line, having sex with their students.

We rarely talk about the conditions of teaching—the isolation, the combination of extreme expectations and strange contempt—as common denominators. We focus on the age difference and a simple binary equation: the teacher as a power figure and the student as powerless and passive. (Nevermind that power can shift inside classrooms, or that students themselves can express sexual desire, can bully or intimidate.) We can repeat the details of abusers' dysfunctional backgrounds, whether someone was hyper-religious or irreligious or doped up on drugs. Somebody always uses the word "pedophilia," so easy to attach to crazy people, so easy not to attach to oneself. But don't I get off sometimes from the attention students give me? Don't I enjoy their neediness as much as I dread it? Don't I think, sometimes, that there's one fresh face who understands me in a way I love to pretend is new?

We don't seem able yet to acknowledge that such dynamics can easily slip between healthy and incredibly destructive.

I remember my second year teaching high school when I picked up a loose textbook sprawled open on the floor behind a desk and returned it to the beat-up shelf where it belonged. But holding the book, I noticed something else. When the pages were closed together, there were words visible on the collective edge, a dark pencil zigzag spelling out: *I fucked Miss Scott.* Even as I scrubbed the words with a pink eraser, I wondered (horrified? curious? flattered?) who had written the message. But I was also relieved that the message didn't say *No one fucks Miss Scott.*

I think about Mary Kay, in the moments when she must have enjoyed being a teacher. What was it in her training as daughter-sister-wife-mommy-teacher that taught her a twelve year-old boy would make her perfect soul-match?

Did Mary Kay really believe this boy was so much older and wiser than his twelve years of life—or did she in fact still fancy herself, deep down, as a little girl?

July 9: After lunch

Late coming back this afternoon because I ran home to look up a picture of Mary Kay online. Her face is everywhere if you look for it, maybe because Mary Kay the schoolteacher-lover-rapist has a Cinderella face and blond hair. She seems to be the wet dream of cultural fantasies about teachers, the opposite of the frustrated wrinkly hag: young, pretty in plaid jumpers or blue jeans, spontaneous and smiling; she could pass for single even though she's safely married with four little children. She is the fun mother, the good friend, the indulgent sister.

But she forgets to clean shit from the cat litter once in a while, then a lot. She'd rather have fun, make messes cutting and pasting with the kids and then leaving the mess and not cleaning it up. There are accounts of her loving pregnancy but not liking the actual work of raising children. At her first and only teaching job, she blew off meetings, and people let her get away with other professional problems because she was *so so so* enthusiastic about the kids, so smiley and excited all the time. I found one report that recounted her ritual at the beginning of each class. Some education professor had told her to offer students *H H or H* every morning: Hug, Handshake, or High Five. To connect, she said.

In her glowing face, I just see a girl. If she were teaching high school, she'd get one of those pseudo awards like "most likely to be mistaken for a student." (I got that award my second year teaching.)

She could be named after the famous cosmetic maker, the one whose salesladies drive blush-pink Cadillacs.

July 9: Evening

It's almost as if we're stuck in the sessions this week, playing at sixth grade. People who run things keep telling us we "deserve" this time—yet there's an element of pretend that feels like child silliness, way past its expiration date and not something to which I want to return. Thinking back, I was sometimes mean in sixth grade. I was heavy but I didn't yet wear a bra or shave my legs. My teeth were growing in crooked. Boys that had liked me suddenly didn't like me so much anymore. My mom still braided my hair. Seventh grade was a torture of teasing.

I don't want to go back to those years myself, but maybe some teachers do. Maybe Mary Kay thought she was fixing something when she risked her whole future by having an affair with a student. Or maybe she'd deny that she had anything broken that needed to be fixed. Maybe Mary Kay had a better junior high experience than most of us—maybe that was her big problem.

Certainly a teacher who's feeling broken or starved for affection isn't always the best (or safest) guide or mentor. Only a sadist would make hunger victims serve famished customers at a buffet table. Talk about a formula for violence, for violation. The simple *fantasy* of nutrition—physical, emotional, intellectual, or sexual—can't sustain anyone for long. Why should teachers be any different?

I remember when a dark-haired colleague of mine, in the midst of some difficult times with the man she'd been living with for several years, framed a photo of herself with an arm around a male student and showed me where she kept the picture in a drawer at home. She shared her romantic dreams about this student: one, where they kissed a little after a sunset drive in the desert; another, where he chased her through a garden and tackled her gently to the ground. When she told me, she flushed and put her hands across her heart as if to hold onto the moment. "In the dream he said he was sweet on me. That's all. Isn't that just romantic though?"

Her relationship with her real-life partner during this period did not improve.

My friend eventually traveled with this kid, along with a few of his friends, as a chaperone on a school trip. She told me they stayed in a hotel, in separate rooms. "Of course," she said. Separate, that is, until she called next door and joined them for the night, sleeping outside the covers on a bed while they crashed on the floor. "We talked all night," she told me, describing it like a slumber party. "About philosophy and things."

Following graduation, two of the boys popped by to visit the school. I overheard them cutting up in the parking lot. "She wants to *Do* us," one of them was laughing—the one my friend referred to as a teddy bear. The ridicule was cruel, perhaps worse that I never told her. But what exactly could I have said that would have helped? (And why do I write this now?)

I thought of their laughter when she complained, later, her eyes hurt and blank, that the guys had stopped contacting her, that the boy whose picture she decided not to keep had seemed to fall from the end of the world, no longer responding to her Christmas presents or email. Maybe deep down she was actually relieved.

There's nothing quite like the goofy adulation from a student in class, nothing more addictive than student loyalty and what might feel like respect and camaraderie. But it's easy to dwell too much on it, to believe in it, crave it, cultivate it, make it our drug. Teachers, too, can be seduced in the containment of classrooms.

To keep that from happening, I think we each need something, anything, that connects us outside the walls. Something to fall in love with and keep up our sleeves, under our skins. Something to call our own.

July 10: Morning

I find myself stuck on Mary Kay, and at the same time I worry somebody here is looking over my shoulder. No one wants to think about the sexuality of female teachers. Popular images suggest that the woman teacher may be sexy in someone else's eyes, and she may be tempting, but she better be harmless in the end—a sweetheart rather than an authority figure. If we challenge her, we'll probably win and she knows it. According to this standard, real female authority, if it exists, comes off frustrated and sour—"She's not getting any," kids will mumble about a cranky teacher. "She just needs a good screw."

In one picture I've seen, Mary Kay smiles like Minnie Mouse on the shoulder of a brooding Vili Fualaau, tan and muscular with proudly arced brows. In the pose, she actually looks smaller than he does. Not an image of our cultural nightmare but a more perverse fantasy: mommy-teacher-sex-kitten all in one. Her eyes look content, fulfilled, and her pose seems flirty and familiar. We say we're horrified by Mary Kay, but maybe it's because we have way too much easy fun judging her. We may call her a rapist, but we actually believe she's a different predator than the typical male coach, teacher, or counselor who abuses his position to get sex. Would he fall in love? No way. He has authority to abuse. Authority? Mary Kay never thought she had any of that. She wanted flowers and unicorns, smiley faces, and I LOVE KIDS, in capital letters.

At the YMCA a few days ago, I heard women on treadmills giggling about the marriage between ex-teacher Letourneau and ex-student Fualaau. An instinct rattled me: Deep down, maybe people believe that when you're a teacher, and a female, you're asking for it. You want it. You give it out for extra credit on your state salary. Even on "Rate My Teacher Dot Com" one primary quality students evaluate is "Easiness."

Fucking figures.

July 10: Afternoon

I've got to take a break from thinking about Mary Kay. But based on her upbringing by a father in the John Birch Society (he actually replaced super-racist George Wallace as Presidential candidate when Wallace was assassinated in 1968), I wonder what she would have thought of today's session. Especially since Vili, underage or not, wasn't the white-Corona-Del-Mar material her father would have preferred.

This morning we looked at ABC's on an overhead transparency from the 1950s. Each letter depicted a chubby cheeked white kid, like from the old Campbell's Soup cartoons, doing some activity associated with the letter. There were some disturbing images — like "B" for "bayonet" and "S" for "soldier," and one of them showed the little kid stepping on what appeared to be a little kid of Japanese ethnicity. People gasped, of course — the *I Can't Believe These Were Actually Used in Classrooms* gasps — and the professor made a connection to some political cartoon from now, someone we're all supposed to agree on as "bad" and "right-wing" — and I just froze up. They talk like we're past all that now, above bad politics, and the contemporary teacher just purges all biases and teaches in a well-adjusted vacuum. Like I've heard teachers say, *I don't see color. I don't see class. I don't see gender. I just see Kids.*

So when we got to this powerful speech from Frederick Douglass, "The Meaning of July Fourth for the Negro," where he uses the language of freedom and patriotism and independence to deconstruct the logic of slave owners and polite intellectuals, no one mentioned any possible contemporary connections of Douglass's argument to Afghanistan and our recent invasion, no one talks about the problem of schools, say, as compulsory spaces. No one says anything that's difficult or upsetting or pushes the discussion further. In a way, we talked *around* the text that we had just read (the way we tend to complain that students do), only coming to bland and generic conclusions: that MLK's "I Have a Dream" speech (the only one anyone seems to read) was very wise, and Vietnam (or whatever else) was very bad, and the Civil Rights Movement was (past tense) great, and everybody's the same now because we've come a long way, Baby. Anything deeper than that means just bothering people. No wonder we can't talk about sex.

Side note that seems important: there's only one woman of color in these workshops.

Here's a bumper sticker most people wouldn't like: WWMKD—What Would Mary Kay Do?

July 10: Evening

I came home pissed off and unable even to talk with Justin about it, feel like time's been wasted this week but now it's too late to fix that. What could I be doing instead, though? I'm undecided. More and more silent inside, feel myself clamping down. Migraine coming. Meds a must.

July 11: Morning

Grogged out and woozy. Colleagues can smell it, seems almost they descend like vultures—here's a relaxation technique, what medication do you take? What time of the month do you get them? I haven't had a migraine in seven years, I hear massage really helps, don't drink that coffee, why did you bother to come today? I try to zone these voices out. No one says, "Hope you feel better."

I'm reminded of the woman who shared her pain in the Author's Chair, and it occurs to me that illness and trauma seem to be the easiest places for teacher women to bond. But this doesn't feel comfortable or healthy. We seem to have a harder time when it comes to sharing or recognizing what we do well—unless we can prove that it connects to our work with students.

As a writing experiment, I'm letting Mary Kay's voice take over. I sense that this character will simplify things for me. *I will read in the Author's Chair this afternoon. Tell them about my brother, how when I was twelve years old we had a party at the house near the beach, a party on the patio by our blue pool. Mother says I don't have to stay in my room today, the usual punishment when I talk back or sneak wine coolers in the garage. Mother likes guests to see me. On the patio by our blue pool, she has hired caramel-colored women to lay cakes and little sandwiches out on a long table. No beer or rum in the sunlight—that comes later. Dad is Orange County proud from re-election. Guests talk Jerry Falwell, house prices, the scandal of rap music. I overhear them telling each other, telling my mother, Mary Kay may be growing up but she's not changed at all, her hair's so pretty, what a perfect little figure, a regular doll, a regular Alice in Wonderland.*

My little brother wears purple swim trunks and crams whole sandwiches in his mouth, then dives into the pool to splash me. Marco Polo, Marco Polo by himself. He dog paddles, seal dives, spits screwy faces my way. I hold a plastic cup of lemonade and try not to think of cakes I want to be eating. A lady doesn't gorge, doesn't guzzle. I dip toes into the pool. My pink toenails, the gold ankle bracelet. Marco Polo. For some reason, I have been staring at the top of the backyard wall, the line where it meets the sky and palm trees, drawing everything together like a big grey thing. And then my father is suddenly in the water, shoes and pants and everything, his silk shirt ballooning up with the slap of air on the water. Mother is shrieking. Someone drops a cup of lemonade. I almost fall, somehow my culottes are soaked. My brother, like my own little cat that follows me to bed when Mother sends me upstairs too proud to break, then I'm crying, usually for eating too much or making the family late for Mass, the drinking (like I said) or talking back. Hands lift my brother from the water – he looks white and tiny on the cement, soaked trunks sucked to his crotch. Why am I embarrassed? Dad crouches, his clothes and hair like wet paper-mâché across his body, and he pushes against my brother's chest, does that kissing motion to get air back in his lungs.

A woman is yelling – "Mary Kay! Mary Kay!" – there's someone yanking one of my arms. I can't hear because I already know. These strangers are only trying to keep my brother, or bring him back. Right then I gorge a whole piece of cake, shove the plate up against my mouth, cake is everywhere on me. The tugging on my arm has stopped and it's quiet except for the sound of people's shoes on the patio, another big grey thing as if years have passed and strangers have discovered it. I gag up the cake nearby in a cactus planter. Men with the gurney come to take his little body away and I can't watch. I sit on the grass next to the planter where I have already puked. I don't pick the dried bits of icing and dough from my cheeks or out of my hair. Marco Polo, Marco Polo. Every single body leaves the patio. I feel it. Every single body. Following the death.

July 11: Afternoon

Again Mary Kay's voice returns: *I was way late to the training meeting today and am getting a few dirty looks but I'm going to write a little anyway, even though they're starting with some discussion about a book I haven't read. I can fake it, I'm sure. I think that some of these activities could even be more fun, like if we worked in a game or two instead of just the activities. Maybe we could do it during the writing time? Writing is so solitary, so unsocial. Also, I notice that the presenters seem to know a few people but not everyone, and they aren't even trying to get to know us. It's not like they need to do H H or H at the doorway, but couldn't they come up with something, some way to show interest in us as individual people?*

I'll show them myself today. I'll read in the Author's Chair.

July 11: Evening

I came home and watched Oprah, *which had already started, and she had a whole audience of pretty women, all different colors, squealing and shrieking. It was like a slumber party during the day, except these were all teachers and Oprah was giving them things. Not lame stuff like books or paperwork for a medical plan or apple-shaped decorations (which I do like sometimes). I mean she was handing out vacations to the tropics, and expensive designer jeans, and sets of face creams, top of the line computers with iPods, bed sets with giant comforters, and this thing I liked the best which was a delicate china tea set with individual pieces shaped like flowers and flower petals.*

I don't know if Oprah was giving these things away because she bought them for all these women herself or if someone had donated them to hand out, or if they were just pure advertising, but it was so great to hear a group of women squealing with delight. Then discovering that these delighted women were teachers, each one representing a different school, from schools all across the country, and knowing that someone thought they should have a few pretty things and a few luxurious opportunities made me feel just happy.

Since I was home alone, I didn't have to leave my husband and the kids like I do at night. I had left all my papers to grade in a pile on my desk at school. I called Vili and picked him up from his mom's and then drove us to the usual spot. He brought a big Whitman's Sampler and we sat in the van with the giant box of crayons and colored in the books I store there for my own kids. And then we drove somewhere else, somewhere safe where I could put on my nightshirt even though it was still daytime and he could watch me, and then we could touch each other.

Outside, it felt like rain but wasn't raining. I miss the heat of the beach some days, those summers at home with my family, my sweet brother. (My brother died when he was three, but I always picture him so much older.) What could I have done for him? But when Vili kissed me, his mouth so small, so gentle, I remembered how I read aloud in the workshop today, read that piece about my brother falling into the water, about my brother drowning, and how some of the women cried. In the end they all applauded me even though they had given me dirty looks when I came in late for lunch. And I realized, kissing Vili back, that everyone understands death. Death makes everyone feel guilty and sorry. Sorry and sad.

Recovering Teacher

The only hope, or else despair,
Lies in the choice of pyre or pyre —
To be redeemed from fire by fire.

— T.S. Eliot, from "Little Gidding"

The Christmas after I broke away from my career teaching English at the public school from which I'd graduated sixteen years earlier, my husband gave me a license plate frame that read, in plain black letters on a silver frame, *Recovering Teacher*.

Although I appreciated his part-silly, part-celebratory gift, I put off attaching the frame for a month or so. Something in the phrase bothered me, sounded bitter or regretful, suggested a distance from teaching that wasn't entirely accurate for me. In the months after screwing the frame in place, I noticed it preoccupied me as I drove. When a car pulled behind me at a stop, did the driver read the message, I wondered? What if I made a poor lane change, ground from one gear into another, or made a hasty left turn at a yellow light? Did the driver blame me more because of the frame, or did he blame me less?

One afternoon, a man called at me across the YMCA parking lot: "*Recovering* teacher?"

I kept moving but looked over my shoulder. "That's right," I said. I was headed to the gym not just for sweat, but for healing and distraction. I was missing someone who had recently died from "un-recovery," a person I hadn't seen in two years.

Neil Webb had been my teacher and my colleague. He was used and eventually discarded by an educational system permeated by the belief that all teachers should be heroic, obedient, and utterly dedicated to their jobs and students every day of their work-lives, often at the expense of their personal lives. But this "perfect teacher" fantasy does not make allowances for imperfection or dissatisfaction. And asking a teacher to perform in this way ignores the passions and ambivalences that draw some people to the profession in the first place.

I left the frame on for three years. It made me think about what it means to "recover" in other contexts: maybe we're all recovering from something? I knew that "recovering *teacher*" might provoke retorts from the average person: *But you get summers off! You have that pushy union! And you work with kids all day — what could be more inspiring?* My license plate frame registered its own small protest against unrecognized and unacknowledged abuse. I know too well how the duplicity of teacher worship can smother those of us who don't fit, those who blatantly fail, and the ones who struggle too little or too hard. Some of us seek rituals to regenerate ourselves, not only to keep our careers but literally to stay alive; some fake the job to keep sane; some get worn down and stay anyway. Some literally suffocate.

Neil died alone in a downtown motel bungalow on an ordinary California Monday. He received no tearful public eulogies, no wooden plaque in the school office, no scholarship funds dedicated in his name. Banished too late from teaching to find the means, or support, to recover, Neil left only the stain of his grief and self-destructiveness for the colleagues and students who loved him, for those who felt a deep isolation in their inability to help him. When news of his death came, each of us huddled alone against the arms of a chair or sofa, whispering to one another on the phone: *He's gone? Mr. Webb? He's really gone?*

From across the street, the Santa Cruz Inn still looks like a romantic, historical find, reconstituted long ago by architect G. Stanley Wilson from a two-story 1920s duplex: narrow French-door balconies, mosaic panels, Moorish archways, Spanish tile roofing, a cement courtyard where a pool could have stood. A protected city property, the Inn stands two blocks from the long hollow but newly reconstructed Fox Theatre where *Gone With the Wind* held its first public screening. Charming from a distance, the Santa Cruz has a local reputation as a halfway house that receives frequent visits from police.

I suspected, before I knew, that Neil Webb had kept a room at the Santa Cruz. After his death, I drove down the narrow alley alongside the Inn for a closer look, then stood in the tight parking lot. I saw the gashed screens peeling back, the scabbed plaster walls, broken windows like chipped teeth, crumbling steps, missing room numbers. Inside, I felt the cloying smell of old smoke and ash, saw the wall of wooden mailboxes, a few stray envelopes, a sticky metal ashtray. When I tapped the broken service bell it merely clicked. A tired Chinese woman appeared and frowned at me. Frowned hard. "Yes, Webb. He drunk," she said. I looked at her stained fingers. "Not die here. No, not here."

A week later, I received the official death certificate, which listed the Inn's street address as Neil's last residence. The room number identified where his body had been found, "on the carpeted floor near the bed." On the phone, the detective told me not to misplace any grief, not to be surprised. Certainly, there had been no foul play, it had been the decedent's own fault—although, he added, "It was real obvious that he suffered, based on the condition of the body." There had been blood on the carpet, and many ants.

Then the coroner's report arrived by mail, a thick sheaf of typed pages. "We don't usually finish these," a county worker had told me on the phone when I requested the documents. "Unless someone asks." Specific statistics aside from Neil's height, age, and weight included the following: 34170, the number on the tag on his right "great toe"; the blood alcohol level of 0.13%; the quarter-inch mustache and three-eighths-inch beard; the five inches of "scalp hair." Select passages from the rest of the report—though technically detailed and detached—read like a kind of medical blessing, tracing his body from head to toe: *There are no fractures of the skull. There are no injuries to the torso. The cranial nerves have normal distributions. The surfaces of the brainstem and cerebellum are unremarkable. The upper airway is not obstructed. The tongue is unremarkable. The bile ducts are unremarkable. The thymus is atrophic. The bone marrow of the ribs and clavicles is unremarkable. The vessels are unremarkable. The calyces and pelves are empty, opening into ureters that maintain a uniform caliber and open into an unremarkable, empty bladder. The esophagus is unremarkable. The small and large intestines and appendix are unremarkable.*

The autopsies that saturate TV programs like *C.S.I.* did not prepare me for the awkward, cold intimacy of such final nakedness. I did not want to be ashamed of looking. I pictured the doctor speaking into a tape recorder as he worked on Neil's body in the mortuary, the transcriber later snapping Double Mint as she adjusted an earpiece and typed the doctor's words into blank spaces on official forms. "Who wants this?" she might have wondered.

Neil's first name was misspelled on every page. The final page, above the doctor's signature, included a list of physical specimens taken from his body for standard toxin screens: bile, gastric contents, brain tissue, liver tissue, and vitreous fluids. His blood, according to the report, was retained in a tube with a purple top.

Words on forms were the last remaining signs of a life I only partially understood. Reading them, holding them in my hands, I wanted to honor and recover, somehow, what had expired long ago.

———

Neil Webb died when I was thirty-five, the age he had been twenty years earlier on the first day I saw him in a classroom. It was his second year working at our school, and he was a teacher of both German and Latin. He scared and fascinated many of us, and former students still refer to "Webb" as both "brilliant" and "weird." Though his hair was fine and beginning to thin out, he wore it long around his face and ears, sometimes letting it fall like an angled cap from a center part above his forehead. His eyes were dark and wedged deep under his eyebrows. His cheeks bunched up into themselves when he smiled and, in profile, his nose resembled Paul Newman's. He moved smoothly and deliberately, like a dancer or cat, and when he gestured with his hands we could see that thick sinews and muscle bound his wrists and forearms. He seemed blatantly indifferent to social pressures of appearance, often wearing the same clothes for days on end. Yellow chalk dust stains became indelible near the pockets of his favorite brown corduroys. One morning he came to class with a chipped front tooth.

There were rumors about his drinking and his private life: *Was he dating one of the counselors? Did he drink before coming to school? Had he ever married? Was he homosexual?* His own stories only fueled our curiosity: when he came to class with his arm in a canvas sling, he advised us never to arm wrestle a woman in bed. We heard that he'd burned down a rental cabin he had lived in. He smelled like tobacco every day, and kids gossiped that they smelled booze, too. He was the first adult I ever heard say the "F" word.

Despite the outward appearance of chaos, I don't think anyone ever doubted that Webb was passionate about the languages he taught, or that he himself was a brilliant student of the subject matter. Sometimes, he would break away from the lame sentence exercise at hand, nudge a soft-cornered copy of *The Iliad* or *The Metamorphoses* from under a stack of papers on his desk, and begin reading to us. His chin poised above the pages, he looked down as if into a lost world. I had a vague sense then that we were witnessing him in an intimate, almost erotic moment, his mouth coaxing the syllables gently aloud, caressing the dead language to life. His apparent frustration with the mundane demands of classroom protocol would slough away until, abruptly, he would thump the book shut again and stride back to the board.

A friend turned to me in the hallway once, adjusting her backpack on a shoulder. "How he reads," she said. "It's the most beautiful thing I've ever heard."

Webb's blackboard notes, like his quizzes and tests, were an immaculate calligraphy — as if he couldn't stand to write anything that didn't at least look beautiful, even if it was the most elementary sentence for translation: *Gallia provincia est. Pueri in agricola sunt.* When addressing us, he exuded formality, always emphasizing the most prominent syllable in our surnames. He might fiercely press the tip of one finger into a word on the board during an exercise: *Would you care to conjugate this verb — Mr. HIS-ten? Mr. Pa-LA-gi? Miss FITH-ian?*

Webb's idiosyncrasies allowed him to embrace "teachable moments." He was famous for singing with his students, and he taught our class the first verse of "Gaudeamus Igitur." Its translation begins, "Let us rejoice while we are young... The earth will cover our bones." As if in a variation on that theme, to explain the Latin verb *"expirare"* and its English derivative "expire," he dragged a dusty record player from a Formica cabinet and slipped the opera *Pagliacci* from its cardboard jacket. Before he eased the needle into the final grooves of the record, he told us to listen for the last breath of the dying character. He wanted us to grasp that "expire" meant "to die," as in to "push out" or "give up" the breath of life.

There were darker flashes, too, when his storminess erupted at what seemed then like random moments. Thinking now, as an adult and fellow teacher, I realize it usually happened when he could no longer endure the glib or indifferent attitude of students, who mumbled that Latin was "stupid" or that they "didn't care" or simply shrugged or stared in silence. At moments like these, reacting to our laughter, Webb might throw one of his shoes against the blackboard, pound the heel of his hand on an open book, or snap, in his own operatic bass, "Quiet!"

By senior year, even though most of us had moved from studying Latin and German to studying Spanish or French, we found ourselves admitting crushes on Mr. Webb. I was shocked most when this whispered truth emerged at a slumber party where, piled around the living room playing a pajama version of Truth or Dare, a friend who didn't even have Webb as a teacher confessed she found him attractive. One by one, down the row of couches and pillows, each of us nodded, then tittered about it.

By the time we graduated, the classes Webb had been teaching were being reduced or phased out; in fact, foreign language programs were gutted throughout California in the eighties. By 1988, just six years after he had started teaching, both Latin and German had been removed from the school curriculum. Mr. Webb was quickly bumped to teach other material, mostly in literature and composition, as if to emphasize the interchangeable nature of subject matter while also disrespecting his primary expertise. Webb had no choice if he wanted to continue teaching, but since he had excelled as a Classics student, a lover of ancient and now-unspoken languages, I can only imagine how deeply he registered the institutional disregard. It must have felt as if someone had forced his head underwater and ordered him to continue breathing.

The autumn after I completed my bachelor's degree, I returned to the school as an English teacher myself and began to interact with Webb as a colleague. I still idolized him, and while it was difficult for several years to call him by his first name, it was even more difficult to cross as a teacher-adult into what seemed a very private world beyond the classroom.

I watched him dunk teabags into the grubby coffee cups he grabbed from a shelf in the teacher's lounge. I saw his hands shake as he stirred hot water with a dirty spoon. Some days I smelled alcohol on his breath and his clothes. I watched him lose weight underneath the same ratty shirts and khaki pants. I overheard co-workers, whom I had also known previously as teachers, whisper and gossip: *Neil doesn't keep a gradebook. His classes are out of control. I feel sorry for his students – they lose a year of instruction. You hear he lost his driver's license? Another D.U.I. What a waste. Remember that I testified for him when they tried to take away his credential?*

He and I shared the same conference period some semesters. He told me about the time his mail got stolen, how it took him months to realize that the culprit had changed his address for bills and bank statements. He rolled his eyes at pompous and basketcase colleagues alike, occasionally throwing in his wildly spot-on impression of William F. Buckley grimacing with a sharpened pencil. Sometimes he told me stories of special meals he had made — corned beef, roasts and puddings, haggis. When I brought cookies to the lounge for teachers to share, his flattery was always specific: "God, you put *real butter* in these!" At other moments, just passing shoulder to shoulder in the hall, something more personal: "What *is* that perfume you're wearing?" He also confided to me, with a surprising lack of creepiness, how he thought that one of our middle-aged colleagues had "such pretty legs."

Some mornings he was withdrawn and didn't want to talk, but even then he held the door for me when we crossed paths. Afternoons, from my perch at the lounge table grading papers near a single, small windowpane, I could see him walk across the faculty parking lot and just off school property, behind a hedge, sneaking privacy and a cigarette or two.

In the years after he could no longer legally drive, he occasionally asked me for a ride home. The fifteen-year-old inside me could hardly believe I got to do this.

In the car, he told me all his good jokes. One, he admitted, had gotten him into trouble with parents. He held up a "V" for Victory sign.

"What's this?" he asked. Like a sprite, he smiled with his eyes.

Of course, I didn't know.

His hand, trembling a little, dropped back to the worn felt of his trousers. "A Roman ordering five beers," he said.

When he did laugh, he produced both snicker and cackle, a fluid timbre that seemed to come from deep beyond his vocal cords. Although it was usually high-pitched, the sound had a depth of breath underneath and an admirable impunity – like the last laugh of an expiring man.

I remember driving him to a little brown house on Coolidge Street in a weedy neighborhood with stray dogs and overgrown trees, all crammed against the edge of some railroad tracks. Rarely did he carry anything home with him, unlike those of us who were always hauling around a roller bag or giant briefcase as if to show to the world that teaching was hard work. Sometimes he had a windbreaker on his lap or a clipped sheaf of student papers. He usually dipped his head and offered a genteel "Thank you" before he got out of the car. Pulling away, I would watch a cat sidle towards one of his ankles when he stopped to peek inside the mailbox.

During the eight and a half years I worked with Webb, his drinking habit got worse. One year, he fell into a construction site, a dug out underpass built to circumvent morning trains in one of the city's busiest intersections. After he injured his ankle in that accident, it became more common to find him reeking of alcohol. I saw a colleague give him a Breath Assure pellet in the hallway one morning, and he accepted the mint with his face to the wall, the tail of his shirt hanging, untucked, like a little kid's.

One of the most demoralizing forms of censure for a veteran teacher is removing him from a central classroom and forcing him to travel from room to room each class period – every hour, five times a day, for five different groups of students. Anyone who has survived traveling even a few periods a day, particularly in disciplines that use lots of books and generate tons of paper, will testify that it's an organizational nightmare. The tactic is usually reserved for brand new teachers or for those troublesome tenured few that administrators want to fire but don't want to confront. The ironic thing is that in deciding to "punish" the teacher this way, especially one who already has problems, administrators help him to fail while putting students in the middle – usually the troubled ones who are themselves most "at risk," the students less likely to care or complain.

Traveling, being made essentially "homeless" at school, was Webb's final demotion after losing a means to impart the languages he loved to teach, then losing access to accelerated or challenging curricula.

I still wonder what might have happened if the school staff, as a community, had confronted Webb years earlier—when he was thirty-five instead of fifty-three. Perhaps this confrontation did happen, when I was too young to see it. Perhaps Webb couldn't bring himself to accept the help. But there might have been additional alternatives. We might have seen him as a struggling human being instead of scapegoating him as the "problem" employee, the exotic and tortured genius who would never fit in, or the pathetic colleague who made us feel less bad about our own problems. Instead, numbed by our isolation and exhausted by our own sacrifices, we took the easier path—feeling angry with, sorry for, amused by, or superior to him.

Like Webb, many of us had ways to numb the stress. At various times I've used: painkillers, fasting, sex with a depressing man, credit card binges. I've picked at a small cut along my hairline to keep it scabbing for months at a time. I've graded too many papers too quickly, as if addicted to some movie image of myself as devoted teacher. Most of us chose and managed coping strategies well enough that they didn't cross—didn't seem to cross—boundaries of health or social grace. Workaholism earns praise, and no one can smell sedatives. Webb never exactly tried to conceal his drinking problem, but our own habits of hiding and not wanting to know seemed to make us complicit in the addiction.

The last day he taught at the school, Webb was pulled into the principal's office. Reportedly, a campus aide ordered to "keep an eye on" Webb had caught him smelling of alcohol and informed administrators. I think we all realized, as Webb must have himself, that it was only a matter of time before someone "official" reported what had been all too real for years. But it was long overdue and, because of that, the abrupt pretense of intervention was false and cruel. It was too late to make much difference, even if the attempt was sincere. A district administrator instructed Webb that he had to take medical leave immediately, check in somewhere for rehabilitation, and report back by a deadline—or lose his job and jeopardize his retirement. I don't think anyone expected him to follow through.

Neil Webb walked away from campus that day, slipping back only once to pick up a stray painting, a stack of records, and a book. He did this one morning before school started, before the halls were teeming with kids. I remember being embarrassed that I had seen him, as he kept his eyes straight ahead, avoiding mine on purpose.

The expiration date of his career arrived without a footnote or a mark on the calendar. But as in the opera *Pagliacci*, the final blow had been struck onstage, inside a play within a play. Those of us in the audience were left wondering how much of the plot we had witnessed, and how much we had managed to avoid, comfortable as we were in our states of willful oblivion.

I became the teacher assigned to teach in Neil Webb's room—number 653—where, as a nervous and anorexic kid, I had adored him. In recent years, to accommodate a wheelchair ramp and railing just outside the room, the original entrance—the one his German and Latin students had come and gone through—had been bricked over. My own students came and went through a new door, at the opposite end of the same wall, but I could still see the clear outline of the old door under the white paint, where the new bricks had gone in. When I told students about it, some would say they could see the outline; others would say they couldn't tell. Some voice usually called out for me to confirm the rumors long in circulation about "Mr. Webb."

"I learned a lot from him," I'd say. "He taught Latin here. Can you believe we used to offer that class?"

"Latin?" Voices would be chattering. "What's Latin?"

After the memorial in San Diego, which I attended with seven of Neil's former colleagues, I decided to see if one of the final rumors was true. I drove to Coolidge Street and pulled up along the curb where I used to drop him off after school. I found a workman walking in and out of the wooden skeleton of a new little house. Even the cement slab looked new.

From the car, I saw a woman across the street on her porch watching over some electronic equipment, old snow skis, and pieces of random furniture. A yard sale.

I pulled on the parking brake and called out to her. "How long since it burned down?"

She enlisted the help of two kids hanging in the yard and moved down her driveway toward the street. "Guess it was last summer," she said.

"You know he died?" I asked. "Just a few weeks ago—in April?" The cruelest month, I realized.

"God." She turned to call behind her. "Kids, Mr. Webb died." I noticed she used the formal designation for his name, and the boy and girl came to her side. She moved herself close to my car. "Anything in the paper?"

I told her: the tiny obit.

"He was my teacher," she said, holding one hand as shade across her forehead. "For German."

We talked as the sun bore down. She told me how the night the house burned, her dog had barked and barked until her husband went to the door and saw the orange flames across the street. The neighbors had to break a window and drag Webb across the sill onto the driveway. He sat on the curb while the house burned but kept getting up to go back inside.

"Maybe he was trying to commit suicide," said the little girl.

The woman batted this idea away. "No, no, honey. He was just really drunk." She looked back to her lawn, where a potential customer examined a boom box.

Neil's house had been a tinderbox, she told me, piled with clutter and bottles of alcohol. "My husband and I took a look after," she said. "And all he had in there to sleep on was like a child's bed."

"You mean a twin?" I asked.

"Smaller than that. With headboard and everything."

I remembered how the minister's sermon at the memorial had been heavy on details of Neil's childhood and devoid of reflections on his adult personality or problems. How the photo imprinted on all the programs had been a grey portrait from his high school years.

The neighbor said Neil had lived in the house with a series of men over the past couple years, each of whom had died off, one by one. From AIDS, she thought. The poignancy of dying men feeling safe, choosing to crash at Neil's house because they had nowhere else to go, hit me hard. Even with all his own problems, he had known something about not rejecting the suffering of others.

I thought of all the rumors, the questions about whom he might have been able to embrace in his short life. I asked, "Were any of these men his lovers?"

She couldn't say. "He kept coming back here, after the fire," she told me finally. "At the end, he had no shoes. He would go into the ashes and drink there. It was kind of scary." She looked up at an oncoming car and backed away a moment to make room. "It smelled really bad for a long time."

"You mean the alcohol?" I asked.

"No," she said. "Just the burning."

As I eased the car down the street, I thought of Neil in those last nine months of life. After the house on Coolidge burned down, he had been broken and bloated and indigent, scraping between motel dives along University Avenue, along Market Street, planting when he could at the Santa Cruz and then returning on foot some nights to haunt the husk of the second home he'd burned down in twenty years. The home where he may have lost friends.

I pictured him sitting on a stub of burned out drywall, swigging a bottle and pushing his heels into the dirt and ash. Not laughing anymore, not even talking to himself. I wondered: When did the teacher inside him die? Had he hoarded that moment, guarding it jealously like a secret wound?

Time offers no guarantee of healing or resurrection. Since removing myself from the school system, abandoning that classroom, the steady paychecks, the people Neil and I had shared for almost two decades, I am less sure of my own recovery than ever. Lately, on those desert evenings when I drift downtown in the car, past the Santa Cruz Inn with its rehabbed windows, its glowing neon "Vacancy" sign beckoning white against red, I think of the room I've never seen, where it wasn't me alone on the floor.

I imagine for Neil what I want someday for myself — a final comfort that might break, unbidden, through all accumulated discomfort and doubt. Perhaps, simply, one sudden memory of valediction: fingertips and palms, cool and soft, along the edges of a face.

How Data Will Save Us

No one warns you about the data.

It actually begins in obvious things, unquestioned givens, like theorems in a geometry proof. Mandatory attendance. Roll call. Head counts. Of course, grades. Points possible. Units of instruction. Credits. Syllabi. Even salary tables. No Money in the Budget. You'd been the student years ago rushing forward in geometry class because you were good at seeing ahead, could visualize the steps towards a proof. It was fifth period, the class right after lunch, when everyone was either too loud or too quiet, the smell of corn nuts and sweat and antsy hunger weighing in the close air, the male teacher putting on his gameshow grin, *Joker's Wild*, for the rough crowd. "I just don't get it," a classmate had said, again. She clawed at her bangs and stared down into numbers, diagrams, arrows, words—a textbook that was water warped, torn, and technically outdated except, well, the Cartesian plane doesn't change year to year. (Maybe that was the first clue, the clue disregarded.) Anyway, the girl sat behind you or beside you and so you turned to help, turned back a page in your own book, maybe edged your desk at an angle, so with this girl the sides of your faces, your shoulders, your open books and pages together made a kind of folded Rorschach imprint—*What does this make you think of? And this? And this?* You were proud to see how the ends of things got to be there. A line. A quadratic equation. A triangle. A tangent. You attributed this skill to some natural aptitude for Getting It.

This pride now vexes. How could you not see what was coming? Or did you see it after all, pretend it wasn't really there? That it wasn't your responsibility or your doing? Data crawled out of walls and blackened AC vents and dropped ceiling panels, up from the tile floor, out of broken and unbroken desks and drawers, shelves and tiles, sharp screws or bent nails poking from where something used to be attached. Came from the fingertip smudges and scuff marks on both sides of doorways—entering, exiting: students and parents, other teachers. In the checkbook, too, your rent payments. The car loan. Miles per gallon. Caught up with you. You were actually begging. By the time you called data by name, it was everywhere. There was not enough.

You were its handmaid.

Tycoons seventy years before had built fortunes on polymers, home appliances, machine guns, TV, and frozen corn, frozen meatloaf. The military industrial complex, economists said. Now you live inside a datatainment-surveillance complex. It's still industrial, still militaristic, but this can't be said aloud. Don't make this equation: data equals advertising, equals progress plus we-know-about-you-what-you-don't. Don't say data equals children. Equals learning. Say something gentler. Say No Child Left Behind.

There had been clues all along, besides that big Cartesian clue you missed. From your first day teaching English in your own classroom—*Joker's Wild*—you inhabit a battle of sheer numbers. The battle between minutes in a day and people you are compelled to accept in your room. People compelled to be there. Body count average equals average daily attendance equals X dollars of school funds per day. The battle of papers, binding you to students like Marley's chains, sometimes the very reason they resent you. The reason you may love them.

You lug that sad stewardess bag crammed with folders, lesson plans, loose papers, transparency film, gradebook with tight metal loops. A laptop or random parts of computer, perhaps a flashlight, dead batteries, extra texts and disks. A granola bar, smashed into a small pocket. Coins you will never count. The pen you keep losing. A Spanish teacher friend asks, "What the hell you got there?" "Paper," you say, "Heavier than you think." You heave its bulk from the car trunk, up the stairs, wrench shoulder and neck. (The handicap elevator? Off limits.) Tug your hernia lifting brown boxes of spiral notebooks – *Journals! Students feel comfortable expressing themselves that way!* Collecting seventy-five notebooks at once means a weekend. Means explaining to the in-laws, some half-baked excuse as if you had a drinking problem. Who could feel like leisurely breakfast Saturday with all those journals waiting? Journals you don't have time to read the way real journals should be read. Journals equal data. Equal evidence.

Better the relatives and neighbors don't know. They think you have special skills, that the school system is lucky to have you: *Wasn't that a great movie, Dear, that* Mr. Holland's Opus?

Time and task passes in pages: mangled, hand-crabbed, whited-out, stapled, penned and penciled, typed and retyped, lined and astro-brite whites. Yet you volunteered – didn't you? – for this distinction. Status grows inside the ritual complaints and suppressions, the so-so-smallness of voices against each other in the lounge, in meetings: *I have five hundred pages to grade this weekend. I'm teaching an extra class period. I have two hundred students every day. It's really fine. I can handle everything.* The battle of chosen overtime – unpaid – and cancelled dinner plans. Your own children left with relatives, eating take-out fried chicken again. Family members looking sideways at you. Your sister saying, *Yeah, I figure that teaching must be a lot like being a student. There's always something to do.* She's pregnant so you don't want to tell her how children, even when they aren't biologically yours, have a way of keeping you from sleeping. (That would just be the data talking, a negative value hiding in plain sight.)

Another voice intrudes, a screenwriter you've met: *Are there moments when you just get too close? Too close to the work? To the kids?* Hours numbed in front of TV. Anything but tallying scores, marking for notice, scratching comments on sticky pads. Reminders multiply so much they only remind that you should be reminded. Practicing a formal lecture, preparing for the "teaching moment," click-click programming the computer presentation or smudging notes for the overhead. Anything but answering the phone.

If only school could be a kind of video game. Somewhere voices were praying those words, somewhere a god listening. If only school could be a kind of video game. And then it was.

Start the clock. Put down your pencils. The principal one year saying, hands folded behind his back, as if he were proud of this, as if he'd worked a long time preparing the line: *We know teachers prefer reduced class sizes, but if test scores don't improve, I can't see keeping it a priority.* As if twenty students per class were some get-out-of-working scheme—as if the students loved being smashed together elbow to forearm. *(What does this make you think of? And this? And this?)*

Screw it, you thought without whimpering, here is how the world ends. You started morphing strings of numbers in your head. Lay awake picturing and re-picturing them. Four out of ten, seven out of ten, eighty-three point seven percent average. Pounds weighed. Sizes worn. Calories eaten. Tables published in the newspapers—by test companies bought years ago by info-data-financial-surveillance corporations. (Data tycoons, remember, bored by frozen broccoli and bomber engines?) Each school a number in relation to another school with its number. Each district a number in relation to another district with its number, and the state and county with their numbers. No wonder "school" really means stock market, means real estate. Of course the students learn quickly, whether they pass or fail: *What's my grade now? Now? Now? Now?*

Produce the right scores or don't. Follow directions or don't. Let the data rock you like a sonic boom. Take envelopes and catalogs from your mailbox in the office where there are a hundred mailboxes filled with envelopes and catalogs. Browse, clip coupons for supplies. Order apple-shaped erasers for the classroom. Smile. Keep receipts for money you've spent on the children, who are really someone else's children, so you can deduct some fraction of those expenses. Be thankful, grateful the hallways are not lined with men in gas masks and camouflage uniforms, poising machine guns, be grateful your fellow teachers don't walk the hallways with bruised and battered ankles. Holy, this privilege of scrutiny without violence. Let automation into your heart.

When, holding open a folder, a man or woman in a rayon suit comes to the door demanding pages where students have scratched their names, sentences, paragraphs—when this man or woman offers to score those pages automatically, overnight them to India for cheap transcription by men and women whose chapped brown hands remain untouchable according to religion and law, whose cheap transcriptions will be given numbers by machines and returned to you page by page in a padded yellow envelope the very next day—at this moment, there will be nothing left to protest. You won't think to mention that the caseload of human beings itself has been the problem. That numbers have become too sacred. No one will ask. Someone may place a hand on your shoulder, as if making a blessing. Someone may say, *Work smarter not harder. Don't take this so seriously.* How could anyone stop this undertow? You never technically agreed, never actually said, *I see how data will save us.* But you see now how data will save us.

Half-Hour Lunch

Snacks wait at ends of hallways, inside black-grilled dispensers: stimulations of craving what becomes most wanted. Pray machines won't devour coins or bills. Curse when money disappears, when a wrapper gets stuck on its way down, hangs shiny mockery in full view. There's sadness in eating at school. Sadness in not eating, in cues to eat, hungry-or-not, now-or-never. The industrial bell signals lunch break, nutrition break, passing period. This is the suburbs. It's the inner city. It's the inner city inside the suburbs. Food gets hidden away before and after those bells, hoarded, slipped into backpacks, sweatshirts, purses. Sneaked in. Like drugs or weapons. Student points a chicken strip or quesadilla instead of an index finger, a blade or gun, instead of voicing interesting complaints or reaching for a napkin. Learns to compensate. To stuff it. Teachers who can't stop moving begin class with bagel in hand, a giant mug of coffee, or Big Gulp of soda. "Put that food away," they tell the kids. "When you've got this job, then you can eat in class, too."

School food breeds strange violence, conditions and repeats binge-purge rhythms. *I have no time to eat. I want to eat all the time.*

Still, the newspapers wonder: Where do bullies come from?

Salivating and fidgeting hide the sadness. The bell rules, its gentle brutality internalized like a biological fact—interrupting and pre-interrupting all day. Anything in its path: girl bending to sip from water fountain, boy copying geometry theorems, men screwing parts in a broken copy machine, girl frantic for toilet paper to wrap her first maxi-pad, teacher explaining a paragraph. So with food, with lunchtime. The bell conflates hunger and movement, makes them indistinguishable. Ring as the child takes first bite of sandwich. As he comes finally to the front of the lunch counter, ready for his turn. No student escapes this lesson. No teacher escapes, absorbing exactly how the half-hour lunch is truly ten, maybe fifteen, minutes. Less if there's a make-up quiz to proctor, a parent meeting, advice for a student or two (or three, or ten), any small personal emergency. Cravings turn subliminal for everyone on campus. *Salivate. Fidget.* Frustration tightens eyelids, tired ankles, a sore bladder, or else spills blatantly open—haste, haste—on a binder of notes. Wiped up.

One solution is constant eating. Another? Not eating at all.

There are public lamentations—the news carries bulletins and artists make movies: the processed and over-processed ingredients, refined sugars, trans fat content, microwaves and plastics, overcooking under heat lamps. Brand loyalty exploitation by snack and beverage labels: Doritos, Coke, Gatorade, Snickers. (Why should school food be different from food everywhere else in America?) You don't hear what else stokes the lingering hunger and edgy boredom: this smash-smash of abundance and speed, binge and purge. Anesthesia of "meal" and "meaning."

Sidenote: You are a teacher in a meeting to discuss textbooks. At first all anyone talks about is what the textbook marketers will feed you—filet mignon? salmon pâté? One woman gushes that, last time, the salespeople stood in the doorway with a tray of plastic wine glasses asking: *Red or white? Red or white?* This corporation knows how to treat you, knows what moves teachers, she says.

Perhaps the details can't be what they seem. You live and work here, you get a little crazy paying attention, a little prone to exaggerate. There must be tablecloths somewhere? Linen napkins? Someone taking his time to dry fresh greens with a paper towel? Women whisking a light marinade or special dressing in a tin bowl?

A scene: cafeteria adjacent to a huge fiberglass awning, shading parallel stretches of grey picnic table bolted to the asphalt. Metal rails separate five lines in front of cafeteria windows (for cold food), and two lines through the actual kitchen (for hot food). Kiosks here and there: hot dog carts with bent umbrellas, "national chain" pizza and taco lean-tos, iceboxes on wheels and brimming with popsicles, frozen yogurts. Few humans sit on picnic tabletops, on low steps near close-by buildings. Mostly you mill about under midday sun, move from somewhere to the cafeteria to somewhere else, edge yourselves under narrow eaves in a bold rain, huddle and nibble, scarf and drip your food. The roar of talk-eating. Waiting for time to be up. Maybe a girl squeals. Boys dash, squirting carbonated drinks from plastic bottles at each other, across a dead patch of lawn near a broken drain. Someone slips and falls. Spotty laughter.

As for actual food, you dig into paper bags or cold packs brought from home. Banana. Wilted ham sandwich and slice of cheese. Maybe homemade cookies that can't be finished. Or you pick at foods purchased from cafeteria or kiosks on small foam trays — soggy paper cups weighed down with coleslaw or industrial green salad, cold refried beans, hot dogs, hamburger-shaped sandwiches in silver foil, flaccid pepperoni pizza squares, sweaty donuts. Nacho chips with cheese blurped from a giant plastic tub. Even healthier items — greyish green beans, jaundiced corn niblets, a grainy apple — serve up the degree of demanded ugliness. Your most appealing foods are least healthy, bright and smartly wrapped things from some factory a world away. Hook your fingers around two or three items at once in the race to polish off shiny bags of chips or crackers, glossy candies, bolt down yellow cakes filled with cream. Sweetness.

As with study, cramming is the thing. Perhaps you eat nothing — on strike, maybe. *I am hungry for multitudes. I cannot be satisfied. I cannot stop moving. Will no one stop moving?* Teachers, the smart ones, hide inside — waiting to absorb the frustration student bodies will bring back with them. The sadness that will soon register as squirminess, defiance, sleepiness.

End of lunch bell cues the final sadness, not quite visible until the lope *en masse* begins back to the industrial buildings, the classroom bunkers. At first, you see a napkin here or there, a torn plastic baggie, a foam tray. Suddenly it's everywhere: wrappers, napkins, smeared sandwich meat and torn bread, smirks of ketchup, half-eaten pears, pizza crusts. Red candies stuck into formation on cement steps. Straws and straw wrappers. Defecations of French fries or chocolate pieces. Paper cups, cans, and crushed bottles. All left behind as if it hadn't been real in the first place, as if this were never even the pretense of a meal. Seagulls dive-bomb remains with their beaks open. Circling back, they shit from the air.

When you are young and ignorant, newly teaching, you notice this scene right away. From a distance, you can barely see grass or cement after lunch. You watch students walk away from bag lunches they have barely finished. A principal stands by, holding a walkie-talkie, saying nothing. Maybe someone tosses a perfect banana onto the grass near the trashcan. There's a lot of trash near the trashcans. At least no one is fighting today.

So you ask: *Why do you do this? How can you leave things this way?*

It's the janitors, a girl says. *It's their job to clean up.*

You picture the gulls, realize the girl's heard this line somewhere else. All of them have heard it somewhere else. You imagine the brown men outside now in their green jumpsuits or stained T-shirts and grey pants, lolling garbage cans and scraping detritus with a rake.

You think of the bribery that goes on. Give students gum, it promotes concentration. Give them donuts and juice before a test. If they behave and turn in homework, set a day aside to pile up chip bags, salsa, barely reheated dishes from home. Pile them all on a long table in the middle of the room. If they behave and turn in homework, toss them pieces of candy.

It's their job to clean it up, the girl says again. *They're paid to do it.* She repeats because she thinks you don't get her meaning—that "they" means anyone else, anyone but her. It probably means you.

You let it go. She parrots words that make this place into this place.

You couldn't blame students for lighting fires and saying it's someone else's job to put them out (although this does happen sometimes, in trash cans. Or else someone hits the alarm bell as a false alarm, a prank. You hate these, but have to admit alarms should probably be going off constantly.)

But it's someone else's job to notice—you're just the teacher after all, your pretty little head is tired. You do the math anyway, calculate the ratio of humans to lunch minutes: 350 bodies for every 3 minutes of lunch time. The ratio of humans to bathrooms: 600 bodies for every 1 bathroom. You think of children in faraway cities after a bombing, a tsunami, drastic earthquake, a famine, a flood, how the children poke sticks through mounds of trash to find anything edible, a hole to bury their waste inside. How they might hit each other with sticks to pass time.

You think of the gulls, the janitor men with their rakes. How this place has been made for trashing. How even the best students have learned to practice orphanhood and homelessness. Even you.

Domestic Order Suite

The power of the dominant ideology is always domesticating,
and when we are touched and deformed by it we become
ambiguous and indecisive.
— Paulo Freire, *Teachers as Cultural Workers*

I.

When you see the girl assaulted in the parking lot, you must not come forward. The girl already knows this rule. The law says you teach in the place of parents, but people look at you and see: nailbiting, cardigan sweater, clipboard-in-hand, hair-in-a-bun. Didn't you dislike the alleged perpetrator? Wasn't he the one caught jamming nails and screws into your car tailpipe last spring? Didn't you already report him for skulking around your classroom—something about casting "smug looks" at you? Besides, consider cause and effect. The school makes money for his attendance, so he will return to school after his five-day suspension. He will park his mother's green BMW in the usual spot and float through campus hallways—a wronged warrior returned home.

But forget such hypotheticals, because you won't come forward because other cases have taught you well. There was the teacher who jammed his body between the bodies of two kids—one with a knife, one without—saving the life of one student and getting sued by the other. You recall that the teacher's back and shoulder damage was permanent? There was the teacher who received a long letter from a student, a letter naming her as an object of hatred and spelling out how he would "dearly love" to act out his violent thoughts but instead would just repeat them to her over and over. *You're going to teach a long time*, the principal said. *And you can't let them get to you.* (The principal had squeezed a teacher's shoulders at a party, and when she didn't laugh he froze up and frowned and poured himself another martini and went to sit beside his new girlfriend on the porch.) There was also the teacher—this one truly was asking for it—who flipped through pages of student journal assignments and found images of herself: *I will come to your classroom late one night while you're still working. I will smother you in gasoline. I will light your head on fire. I will shit in your mouth.*

You do remember other, minor incidents yourself, how a person kept coming by your closed classroom door and kicking or punching it so hard that some student in a back desk said, *Damn!* And because the kids had no idea what was going on, they laughed among themselves. At a distance, holding a nub of chalk, you saw a kind of humor. You know too well the cloying sound your voice makes in protest, how it seems to come from nowhere. What would it take for them to hear something strong? Not the dog poisoned behind your rose bushes, not your windshield smashed with a crowbar, not your stabbed body, not your home charred to the ground. Your life is made of hearsay. What's real is your hair falling out and turning brittle, your eyesight weakening. What's real is the smell of blood, like wet hamburger, between your legs—and how you keep trying to hide it. How you can't. You scramble for toilet paper and try not to bleed on yourself. This is no place, no time for hysteria.

II.

Keep telling yourself no one will hit you. Seriously. Not the campus supervisor, not the department chairman, not the principal or superintendent or janitor. Your bunker has four cinderblock walls. One small, square window in the metal door's upper corner.

You used to sing Mozart, play oboe, dig up coins and human finger bones on archaeology trips. You wore striped dresses, pointed shoes, lab coats. Then you fell in love, wanted to share your learning. Now you dig through papers made by students—a hundred here, a hundred there—dress not for weather and exploration but bunker temperature. Good bra. Tank top. Thermal shirt. Sweater you can roll up or peel off. But the bunker thermostat reads eighty degrees when cold air blows in, fifty degrees as heat bears down. No one forces you to stay, to accept this vocation. Eight hours a day, here is your starting place. Students enter the room saying *It's too hot* or *It stinks in here.* The bell blares. They keep leaving you in the bunker with the broken thermostat. Colleagues passing by will announce, *At my end of the building the temperature is exactly opposite of here.* You never stray far.

To the dented bathroom stalls and the sink, still a rust-stained trough—cold water only—the cement floor fifty years old. *The lavatory.* It reminds you of being a child, smelling urine near the boys' bathroom. The faculty bathroom has not been modernized though student bathrooms have new stalls, sinks, commodes. (Inspectors visit these bathrooms, not your bathrooms.) You must not resent the students for trashing their bathrooms already. *Lavatories.* There are too few to go around. At least you don't have a urinary tract infection or genital warts or hemorrhoids. You aren't pregnant. No one has hurt you. It's just mucus down the back of your throat, and you expectorate in the trough when you can, or else just swallow. The lack of air circulation is no one's fault, you certainly don't want to be just another scratched LP stuck on complaining about mildew, mold, dust. Why not take better care of yourself: more citrus, vitamin tabs, dawn walks? You can always bring a Swiffer duster, another stash of Kleenex.

Beyond the hallway voices past the lavatory, beyond your own sneezing, you hear it—the desk phone ringing, someone calling— and rush back to your starting place. A new group of students asks, *Why did you think the phone was ringing? It wasn't ringing.* The intercom blasts announcements. A student throws a book across the room. You hear thuds outside your doorway, a yelling voice you recognize: the small boy with big fists. Your bunker door can only be locked from outside. It isn't.

But this is paranoia, you are simply angry at your own raw throat. There's no emergency button on the wall anymore. If you use the phone, there's an office recording—formal, polite—a woman's voice in your ear. If you speak, the voice may say "right away" but it could take an hour, perhaps never. *Remember your Mozart? Your oboe? Your piles of ancient knuckles?* At least you have lights, fluorescent bulbs that seem slightly surgical.

No one sees those moments that train your attention — not the bulbs flickering, not the now-empty drawer where you swear you secured your purse. Use pink work orders for broken cabinets, the sputtering fuse, loose wires under the carpeting. Nothing that happens hurts you. No one is out to get you. Always invent a witness if you can.

III.

What is your employee number? Can you repeat the expected schoolwide learning results? Yes. Do you know the hourly, daily, and month-by-month calendar of lessons? Yes. Have you counted and distributed test packets to students for the day? Yes. Do you take roll on the S.A.S.I. digital system? Yes. Is the system convenient? Yes. Are you a member of the teachers' union? Yes. Are you a member of the district literacy committee? Yes. Have you completed all supervisory duties at sports events for the year? Yes. Do you sponsor a student club? Yes. Did you ride and wave from the club float in the Homecoming parade? Yes. Do you have enough time? Yes. Do you post homework assignments on the internet? Always. Do you answer questions about homework assignments on the internet? Always. Do you give students your home phone number and personal email? Yes. Do you label all lessons with the correct numbers of standardization, both out loud and on the board? Yes. Do you use the SMART Board and PowerPoint software for automated instructional tasks? Yes. Do you implement all SMART Goals each day? Yes. Do you follow all scripted instructional plans? Yes. Do you consider yourself an educated person? Yes. Do you wait seven seconds for student answers after asking questions as indicated by the script? Yes. Do students give answers as indicated by the script? Yes. Have you studied the cohort analysis documents for all students tested at our school? Yes. Have you studied the item analysis documents for all students tested in your classes? Yes.

Have you stopped calculating grades by hand? Yes. Have you stopped hand writing comments on student work? Yes. Do you feel you are more efficient these days? Yes. Do you attend the requisite training sessions on the latest instructional techniques? Yes. Do you enjoy the training? Yes. Do you have more time for shopping, painting your nails, exercise, and trips to Las Vegas? Yes. Is your electronic gradebook linked to the internet? Yes. Do you feel better about your work with us? Yes. Are you standing up straighter? Yes. Do you like how your body looks? Yes. Do students like how your body looks? Yes. Are you having fewer problems with discipline during instructional time? Yes. Is the classroom workplace more quiet overall? Yes. Do you feel safer now? Yes. Are you eating more organic foods? Yes. Are you having more sex with your spouse? Yes. Do you experience orgasm? Yes. Do you feel less guilty enjoying yourself? Yes. Do you feel like part of an instructional family? Yes. Do you report all glitches in the software? Yes. Have you had glitches to report? No. Do you find yourself daydreaming or losing focus? No. Do you ever wish to be somewhere else? No. Do you regret your choice of profession? No. Do you find yourself more or less frustrated with students? Less. Do you find yourself drinking more or less caffeine each day? Less. Do you need tranquilizers to sleep anymore? No. Are you taking depression meds? No. Do parents challenge your authority? No. Do you experience moments of inferiority? No. Do you want anything else from your career? No. For your students? No. For your children? No. For the neighbors' children? No. Do these questions make you feel self-conscious? No. Do you realize that you are a new breed of professional? Yes. Do you understand the social and economic contribution you are making every day? Yes. Would you describe yourself as satisfied, dissatisfied, or other? Yes. Do you have any questions? — Do you have questions? — Any? — Do you? —

Teeth, Leaf, and Tongues

I know where I am, and who, and what day it is. These are the tests, and I am sane. Sanity is a valuable possession; I hoard it the way people once hoarded money. I save it, so I will have enough, when the time comes.

— Margaret Atwood, *The Handmaid's Tale*

I sit at the dining table in panties and T-shirt, deliberately not primping this morning: no rayon suit and tight shoes; no soliloquy, asides, or dialogue at the front of the classroom today; no talking between the aisles or tucked in corners. (Teachers know: even when it's not a stage, it's still a performance.) No papers from students, from the permanent body of other voices — the despair, the frustration ("But Ms. Scott-Coe, I don't see the point!") — none of their words stack-stack-stacked in my bag or cradled in my arms for the dreaded return.

A mess of scribbled and reprinted essay drafts and Post-it reminders lie scattered under my forearms. Air from the AC vent agitates eyelash corners of junk mail and bill slips stuck under coasters. I've read and marked hundreds of papers here for years, but as I work this morning — drafting my own work, with grading in abeyance — I think of meals my husband, Justin, and I share here. Sometimes just green salad and fried cheese sandwiches, other nights something fancier: fettuccini chicken parmesan or maple roasted pork. It's a pleasure to create something for a clear purpose, a definite audience. It's a pleasure that my husband insists he'd starve without me, that what I create gets better every time, that he literally thanks me for cooking.

I write mornings at this table because I want the energy of sensual tangibility, flavors, and plain human appreciation close to where

I'm putting words together. The life of any person's mind can have many undeclared enemies, and whether we mother children or not, whether we ever teach, any writer can learn early the value of midwifery to create safety for the voices of people we love. We also learn this value when we long for, whether we ever fully enjoy, support for our own honest words.

Today there's an op-ed piece in the *Los Angeles Times* by Sandra Tsing Loh, the first real adult writing teacher — the first writer-midwife — I ever had. This was nearly twenty years ago, when I was a student working shifts as a cafeteria cashier at the University of Southern California. In the short article, Loh describes a recent essay she composed and performed for radio broadcast, an essay that led to her abrupt dismissal from a local syndicate of National Public Radio. It doesn't matter that sardonic humor is Loh's gig, or that she had planned for and requested the word "Fuck" bleeped out of her narrative, for stronger effect. It doesn't matter that she is an accomplished writer with a happy marriage (or so it seemed, at the time) and growing children, and that her career will eventually be boosted by the twist of publicity. What comes through in her voice is her stunned disbelief. Underneath the signature sarcasm, she indicates how the sting of the silencing slap isn't so easy to shrug off — even if you're famous, confident, and indignant enough to publicly discuss it.

Why shouldn't *I* feel out of line, inappropriate, when speaking on the page? The newsprint of Loh's essay has smudged off on my fingertips — text reproduced millions of times for readers (and non-readers who simply page through, page past her) in millions of homes. My own excuse for getting stumped, for copping to silence, is certainly not honest. I might say something snarky like, "Who needs another essay about personal experience?" or "Doesn't the world have enough bad books already?" (How I know well the script of student excuses: *I can't write that much; I can't write that little; Tell me what you want me to say.*)

Half-drugged from migraine meds, half-awake, half-naked, I see myself delving again into these pages, attempting to rewrite from halved parts of myself and somehow gather together, guard against dissolving, dividing, collapsing. Yet I realize also that cells must divide in order to make things. Gestation requires division at the microscopic level, a *multiplication* towards a new whole. No self, no voice, exists without dividedness.

I could be a starfish. An earthworm. Cut me in half and I'll breathe twice the air.

Down the hallway, two clocks in different rooms snick at each other, off just a beat, as if they're in an argument, or a race. I find that I'm writing even as I'm worded-out after the weekend's splurge of language for other essays, for a book review, for private letters. Sentences seem jagged, seem to freeze, and I sense my tongue lodged in my lower palate, stuck in a glottal stop.

This isn't writer's block, that tired cliché: It's an intruding awareness of the wall I'm always lodged against, even in productive interludes.

This wall was prepared for many of us—students and teachers, men and women—years before we entered the world. Am I man enough to write my ambivalence? Am I woman enough to speak for myself? The wall of questions seems encasing at times, with deadlines and mundane things (essays, bills, appointments) looming as usual, without explaining the lurking sensation, the undertow, drawing down.

When did words begin to disturb me? It's not the simple tiredness and numbness accumulating after years of sometimes practiced, sometimes posed empathy, the repeated and attempted-to-be-new comments on thousands of student paragraphs. It's not the adult awareness that some day a student may write, quite frankly, how he'd like to see me dead.

I recall, with a strange and sudden gratefulness, that my father will never sit at this table where I work, a table where I am all too happy these days to serve dinner for guests, and for the man I love.

———

I remember meals at home before my father left, how my little sister and I would sit by the kitchen window with our parents at the oak table, how the two of us would stare at our plates or at the melted splatter of cheap candlesticks, move food to our mouths as our dad popped off in lecture form about anything — the stupid women at his office, a stupid car salesman, the stupid traffic. How my mother would chew quietly next to him. My father had no restraint, no self-consciousness of any kind, yet he would kind of bare his teeth sometimes when putting a fork to his lips between words or phrases, as if trying to seem extra mannerly.

Once, my sister bumped a tooth with the tines of her fork, and suddenly Dad launched into another lecture, this time on chewing.

"Here," he said. "See?" And he took a bite with that exaggerated dainty mouth while my mother sighed and watched us, seeming resigned to stay above the fray.

When my sister cried protest, she was dismissed angrily from the table, and I froze in resentment at this person who seemed more and more like an intimate stranger. From that meal onward, it tortured me that I could actually hear his molars bump together inside his primly chewing mouth, even when we ate soft foods like macaroni, mashed potatoes, or rice.

There were other nights, later on, when my mother, sister and I started dinner in the relief of our own company. Maybe Dad had called ahead from work and I'd heard Mom talking to him on the phone: "Okay. Okay. I'll leave some food on the stove."

Whether he called or not, invariably the three of us would just be sitting down, cutting into the cheese steaks or passing the bread basket, when I would see Dad's old Cadillac lumber into the driveway. I'd watch him through the window as he'd lock the car and hitch up the back of his waistband. He strode to the door with that embarrassing walky-talky-size phone in his hand, his totem of new importance.

I remember that such moments felt like falling or crashing down from a high place. That I had no way to say anything about it. And how, as we heard his hand on the screen door, Mom set down her own fork without looking at us, went to the stove or the oven and stirred the pot, uncrinkled foil from a baking dish, set a lid on the counter like a muted cymbal. Without a greeting, Dad took his time rustling around through the hallway into the elsewhere of the small house. Maybe the toilet would flush. My mother placed a serving of food on Dad's plate and sat down with us again, her elbows on the table, chin and mouth covered by her knuckles. My sister and I tried to get lost in our food, pinching individual peas or corn niblets into tiny bits.

Sometimes, I stared at Dad's place: the blue-rimmed plate piled with steaming food, the glass of fresh cola hissing, the empty chair. He might come in and join us. More often, he would return to the kitchen like a sleepy houseguest, reach for the refrigerator door and say something vague, something to suggest that the trouble of a meal was no trouble at all. "Oh. I'm not really hungry," he'd begin. "Do we have any three-bean salad left?"

And as I sat there and seethed at his obliviousness, at his arrogance, I watched my mother's face. She set her mouth and eyes as if to block out the humiliation with a mask of virtue, like a person pretending she can't be hurt. Maybe she said, "Yes" or "Okay, then," and went on with her green beans, asked my sister a question about her day. Sometimes she would clear her own plate from the table, leave my sister and me with our father's plate of food growing lukewarm in front of the empty chair.

I thought then, and for years afterwards, that my mother's silence was dignified. I wonder now if she put on the sad mask of many women who try to survive disrespect by ignoring it.

What I wanted then, what I want now, is the safety of multiple voices, strange or at-times singular voices coming from different corners of our palates, our lips making different shapes. I wanted somehow to undo a misconception in our household that girls and grown women must wire themselves to a pretense of contentment. It wasn't true that silence trumped speaking up, or that it offered some odd form of leverage — our silences didn't really leverage anything at all.

During those years at the family table, I was taught that an open mouth only leads to "complaining." And complaining could never be acceptable as long as my father was around. As long as my mother remained married to him.

Even so much later — after my father has been truant for twenty years, after I have discovered a healthy marriage and renewed my sense of professional purpose — I still sometimes flinch internally, as if I expect something to strike when I say what I really mean: *I'm not sure I want to be a parent. I am drawn by the human capacity for cruelty, for violence, for survival. I have despised blithe and glib dismissals directed at people who teach.* The flinch comes most sharply when I'm taking a stand, explaining an idea, anticipating potential disbelief, hostility, or questions. I have learned to be over-cautious, over-politic, perhaps simply hasty, as if using too many voices to compensate for the one I'm not sure I've found.

Nearby lies the latest draft of a commentary I've finished that will run in the *LA Times* exactly one week after Sandra Tsing Loh's piece about her own experience with crossing the line. I worry less about whether I like what I've said than: *What will happen if someone disagrees with me? What will happen if I've made a mistake? How can I prepare for my own words to be used against me?*

Sometimes, in such binges of carefulness, it becomes difficult to tell truth from lies.

In her 1989 essay "Talking Back," bell hooks describes the "maddening" effects of the silence demanded in her own childhood. She writes, "Even after publishing books...I had not completely let go of the fear of saying the wrong thing, of being punished. Somewhere in the deep recesses of my mind, I believed I could avoid both responsibility and punishment if I did not declare myself a writer."

Yes, I play this way, too. To alleviate my anxiety, I might fidget and use this pen to clink out a heartbeat on the handle of a coffee mug — *bink BINK!* The grains of wood in the table's surface look now like cutoffs from a failed lie detector test. The jagged scrims and scratches seem unreadable, hacked and re-intersected together. I wonder how many of these grains are even real, if an artisan etched some threads into the wood for a "more authentic" appearance.

Still, my own lies, their internally seismic tremors, draw closer. I am long tired of tidying up for inspection. Yet every day, there are dead ends to scrape away like yellow leaves, like the scrims of fingernail and dry skin we clip and peel from our own bodies to make room for what's new.

I imagine dinner with Justin tonight at this table, how afterwards we will lay pages next to the plates and explore the edits and re-edits I need to complete. How he will nudge me towards talk about what I'd rather leave in a pile of papers. How I need this from him, even though I fight in silence at first.

Why such relief to speak?

He will clear the plates from the table, stack and rinse them near the sink. He will take my new draft to the backyard and sit down on the bench under the myrtle tree, hunch over the paragraphs, read them slowly and smoke (in those days he was still smoking), sketch notes and chew the end of his pen.

Some edits, some forms of cleanup, are far from cosmetic or simply "literary." Sometimes we can actually push forward a new way of speaking when we know someone listens, ready to catch whatever emerges, the way we might need. Our best, then — our most beautiful, maybe — comes in returning the favor, serving as midwives for someone else's expression with our own spoken, written, or silent assistance. When I was teaching all day, every day, this was part of what I'd struggled to do, imperfectly, something not every student welcomed. And ah, how I begrudged that effort sometimes, anxious that my own umbilical connections to silence would gag me in the end.

At the window, there's a green plant I potted last year, its poor limbs wilting regardless of how much I have or haven't watered it. I could snap one of the large, mottled leafs from the stem. I could fold my long fingers into a church steeple and doorway, the way I did as a little girl passing time. I could tuck the leaf under my thumbs. Here could be the perfect place for a glib American ending, the moment where a piece of the natural world stands in as a metaphor to gloss the tricky problems: *Maternal nature listens. Wilted limbs become part of earth. Silence is another form of speaking.*

On a healthy day, I'm a writing teacher still seeking the right to write. My own creativity is distinct from — yet related to — the enterprise of assisting voices that aren't mine, voices I won't own, into some circle of conversation: *My persona is lesbian. My main character is a father who uses his children. My character isn't sure that the Ivy League is all it's cracked up to be. My character has a problem with drinking. All I want are the words I need to start a better conclusion.* When I choose to work in a classroom now, it's not the catchall of "English" or "Language Arts." The class is more consensual, elective, or else so necessary for remediation that the collective desire to move forward can become its own kinetic force. I rarely have more than thirty students at a time — a drastic contrast from my colleagues who still survive teaching hundreds of human beings every day, hour by hour.

And there's still that reminder: the dead leaf that could be like a yellow tongue under my thumbs, stuck in the church doorway made of my own quiet fingers. I imagine pressing into the leaf's spine and plying open a hole, splitting the leaf up the middle. There could be two halves, two new tongues, which fall apart into my lap. Here could be a new outward sign, maybe, a small sacrament of anti-paralysis.

Wouldn't that be beautiful? From the shelves just behind me, I could slip a cookbook from the stack, a volume I never use, and slide the mottled pieces of leaf between some pages.

There is no final word. I still wonder what hangs at the edges, what the students will never want to tell me. I have not yet told them how Justin and I put a suffering animal to sleep last week, a cat who has been my companion since the first day I worked as a teacher. How I watched the vet slip a needle of reddish fluid into one hind leg and saw how his feline eyes didn't close when his heart stopped beating. I laid my hand on the belly of this animal and recalled that it was the birthday of another dead friend, a former teacher and colleague. Someone who died alone, leaving a smudge of his own blood on the drab carpeting of a downtown motel room.

I haven't told my students that Justin and I wanted to bury the cat at home. How, in a strip of earth next to the house, we clawed at the dense ground, thumped the clay layers with a pickaxe, then with the back end of a hammer. It took a long time to make a hole just two feet deep. We felt our weakness in the lame struggle to place this creature in the earth. It had seemed, in our idea of digging, such a straightforward task.

Teach who I am? I plant pink and purple flowers on the black mound the morning after we fill the hole. I dig slots into the soil with a silver trowel and ease each bloom and root where it seems to fit. I cannot spell the names of the flowers here, cannot give a lecture or an explanation of the steps I take to ensure that the blossoms will thrive. Perhaps I have no standards. But I hang chimes nearby on the house, under an intersection of eaves. Five metal rods wait for the air to move them against one another, to play along one chord in the octave of "A."

The Recesses of High School

I have seen my face in the black metal
felt the heat
breathed gray dust hanging
in the air.

This kid knows
what makes Saturday night special.

— Donna Hilbert, from *"This Gun Is Real"*

In the film *Grosse Pointe Blank* (1997), John Cusack's hitman character, Martin Blank, slips on a grim black suit and returns to the nightmare of his high school's ten-year reunion. Repeatedly, he identifies himself as a "professional killer," and on each occasion he lets the phrase hang in the air, dark eyes watching for the moniker to register as something other than a snide joke. "You get dental with that?" one former classmate chirps. The father of his love interest merely tips his brandy glass and notes that it sounds like a growth industry.

I cringe while laughing at these punchlines, at their prescient awareness of easy American denials in the face of local violence. It's no shock that when twenty-four hour cable coverage of the 1999 Columbine horror show overexposed Americans to the then-deadliest school rampage on public record, other sites of similar violence had long slipped from memory. But the names of cities and towns make a very real roster, like clues on some kind of rigged U.S. geography test: Olean (1974), Las Vegas (1982), Manchester (1983), Goddard (1985), Lewiston (1986), Virginia Beach (1988), Olivehurst and Great Barrington (1992), Grayson (1993), Blackville and Lynnville (1995), Moses Lake (1996), Bethel, Pearl, Paducah, and Stamps (1997), Westside, Edinboro, and Springfield (1998), Notus (1999). Then, following the Columbine shootings in Littleton: Conyers, Philadelphia, Deming, and Fort Gibson (1999), Flint and Lake Worth

(2000), Santee, Williamsport, and El Cajon (2001), Red Lake and Jacksboro (2005), Cazenovia (2006), Tacoma and Blacksburg (2007) — the last, at Virginia Tech, on a university campus, with results even deadlier than Columbine.

And now Dekalb and Oxnard (2008).

It doesn't matter that rampage shootings are statistically rare. From 1974 to 2006, the U.S. averaged one per year. Figures don't generally include outsider-initiated attacks by gang members or other individuals*, accidents, assaults involving weapons other than guns, nonfatal shootings**, sexual assaults or mere threats. Stats also don't include "obscure" incidents buried by city or school district public relations machines, and tragedies on college campuses (until recently) were considered separate cases. At my Southern California high school *alma mater* – a "good" school with a green lawn where I also spent half a career as a teacher—one young man committed suicide by gunshot in a carpeted classroom in the early eighties. Our tragedy didn't merit a place in the national chronology, yet I doubt that we hold some unique local skill in masking our worst secrets. Like most anonymous places, we cling to the notion that we must be an oasis.

It Can't Happen Here, we think. *Not in this school, during the happiest days of our lives. Not in the garden of young adulthood.*

Yet autumn rhythms indicate a different kind of awareness, revealing how closely school days link to the macabre in popular American imagination. In one recent Staples promotion for back-to-school supplies, a wrinkly Alice Cooper chides his Goth-looking daughter in the checkout line. Marketers make sure the rush for pencils, paper, and lunchboxes coincides with the placement of Halloween costumes, masks, and orange-black candies on drugstore shelves.

* For example, the notorious shooting in Bailey, Colorado, and its copycat crime in the Amish village of Paradise, Pennsylvania, were committed within a week of each other on the cusp of September-October 2006 . Both shootings were initiated by outsider adult males, not students.

** Some incidents straddle categories. The October 2007 shooting in Cleveland, Ohio, was committed by a student who shot five people but only successfully killed himself.

Our Columbine-Virginia Tech nightmares are a slight variation, because the victimizers don't cover their faces with hockey masks. We may recognize the skinny-shouldered boy with braces, the small harmless blond with acne scars. In jesters' caps or flak jackets they may actually google their eyes, mug and wave for security cameras or their own videotapes as they brandish weapons. (Seung-Hui Cho, the shooter at Virginia Tech, actually mailed his ranting video rationale to NBC between the two shootings on the campus.) Viewers see young men who have transformed hurt, despair, or isolation into active rage—at themselves, at a culture which ignores them except as targets of a marketing ploy, a sales pitch repeating they can have *everything*, if only they pay, borrow, or steal the right price.

There's something else, too: a kind of national catharsis each time, as if the shootings enact some collective dread of school we are not allowed to articulate without clichés, along with a hatred of the in-crowd, resentment of bad teachers and unfair grades, mandatory attendance laws, the ever-tightening straightjacket of standardization. Do we at once pity and fear the shooters as persecuted outsiders—the way we may fancy our younger selves as sad and misunderstood, with nothing to lose or gain inside the too-small universe of school? Do the shootings play out a trigger-happy fantasy we love to pretend we deplore?

Perhaps we cloak ourselves differently, hide inside what's most obvious and therefore feels most righteous: *I had problems, I hated school but I never killed anyone.*

When I was still teaching high school, I dreaded this attitude most—its latent dismissal and hostility burrowed deep inside the fissures of compulsory education. Where does damage go when it goes underground? We deserved better. We know we owe kids more. And we'd just as soon suppress any reminders.

———

The year before he opened fire on his Kentucky high school in 1997, Michael Carneal composed a long story for an English class. In

"The Halloween Surprise," he used his own name and the names of fellow students, describing how he would torture and kill them— crucifixion on a hot metal cross, penetration by heated drill bits, evisceration-rape by a long pole screwed into the ground. In the last sentence, he described presenting the pile of bodies as a special gift to his mother.

Katherine S. Newman's *Rampage: The Social Roots of School Shootings* (2004) preserves crucial legal and personal details of the Carneal case. According to records from civil proceedings after the shooting (who knew this could happen? who is to blame?), the young female teacher who received Carneal's Halloween story admitted no memory of it, and further declared that she probably wouldn't have known whether or not to read the piece as a sign for concern. Perhaps we like to assume the tragedy could have been averted in some way had she simply presented Carneal's ghoulish writing to a campus administrator and sought support. In fact, I wonder if she had done precisely that, but was encouraged in the wake of blood (by district officials, by lawyers) to deny it.

Support for those closest to reading the warning signs may not always be forthcoming. Two years ago, a teacher showed up at my doorstep one autumn evening, clutching at a scribbled piece of student writing on the usual blue-lined notebook paper. A young man addressed her directly in the note, identifying her by name, along with two other female teachers, and describing how he hated her most because she was "a professor wannabe" and he relished thoughts of "doing something" to her. What most disturbed the teacher was how the principal shrugged it all off. "It's freedom of speech," he told her. He removed the student from her class and put him in another (female) teacher's room. That was it. I went with her to the police station to report the student's note. Nothing else happened, but she said she felt a little better knowing there was a formal record.

Inconsistent consequences send inconsistent messages, so that teachers themselves may learn to embrace the dissonance. Another teacher confessed to me that he won't teach summer school again. The last time he did, he confiscated a chain letter three boys were passing around in which they describe knocking him, the "gay faggot" teacher, down the stairs and kicking his head in. The students were removed from summer school, but there were no consequences for the regular school year because the discipline administrator decided there had been no indication of credible threat. If there had been no threat, then why expel them from summer school at all? The teacher was exasperated. "What do they need for it to really matter?" he said. "My cold body on the tile floor?"

I flash back to a day almost twenty years ago, my second year teaching, when a young man slipped in late to class and took a desk at the rear of the packed classroom, proceeding quietly to distract a cluster of students in a back corner. I saw him showing off a cream-colored plastic band under the hem of his trousers, some kind of anklet. After class, when I poked my head out into the grey hallway and asked a campus aide about it all, he said, "Oh, yeah. He's on house arrest for attempted murder."

That's the kind of statement that doesn't even sound real, and since I had received no notification, how could I tell for sure? I was a neophyte with thirty-five other kids in the room, a hundred fifty more coming later that day. The kid brandishing the anklet would return tomorrow. Was I supposed to play oblivious? Invite him to show and tell? When I confronted the discipline administrator that morning and asked her what was happening, why no one had informed me, how was this even legal, all she said was: "We didn't know. We really didn't know about it. We're sorry. Let us know if you have any problems."

The sheer offhandedness offended me most, rendering my question about the anklet and alleged attempted murder as equivalent to concern about chronic tardiness or scribbles in permanent marker on a desktop. What were the students who had seen the anklet supposed to think? What did they tell, or not tell, their parents?

What did the boy himself think of the fumbling adults around him?

I taught nine more years and watched as other, similar incidents added up over time, creating a kind of cumulative flinch-reflex among teachers, four out of five of whom happen to be women. In the recesses of high school, I discovered the perverse logic of retreat. I saw myself as part of a teacher culture that adjusted to being ignored or attacked by increasing our thresholds, steeling ourselves, and letting things go. Schools like ours — publicly "respected" schools, most likely to escape or evade social scrutiny — somehow learn to abort or deny these conversations, and instead communicate a kind of exhausted silence about troubled students.

You'll have to do something more drastic than that, we seem to say. *We don't even hear you yet.*

Kids absorb adult indifference, and in recent studies many indicate feeling unprotected by teachers, even though statistics also suggest that schools on the whole are now safer than ever. (How could students know that teachers themselves often feel unprotected, unsupported, and alone?) Young people clearly perceive instructors' hands-tied vulnerability and sense the political carefulness (i.e. fear of lawsuits) in school institutions. Perhaps they also intuit that teachers' voices don't carry serious weight in the wider, real-world community.

Newman's study of particular school shooting sprees discovered that hints or outright declarations of anger and threats made by Carneal and other young men were largely ignored or passed over until their violence became real. Twenty-one out of twenty-seven shooters from 1974 to 2001 had "warned" someone, often a classmate, though the hint was not taken at face value at the time — and was not usually passed along to any grown-up.

Ten of those perpetrators had composed violent writings or other creative projects such as videotapes or drawings. In some cases, these documents were passed over with a checkmark for credit, were viewed as classroom projects by other kids, or made their way into discipline files or police records. Regardless, from one year to the next, the dots were not connected, and conversations never began. Instead, these kids found other ways to compel our attention.

Ironically, as Newman herself notes, well-meaning confidentiality tends to isolate individual teachers and counselors with burdens no adult should bear without support from a community. Lawsuits following tragedies only underscore the isolation of the teacher-as-witness. *Not here, not my kid, not me.* The inability to speak freely, to air things, hangs over schools like nuclear fallout. Violence and threats of violence make silent detonations in exactly the same atmosphere that generates rules and consequences, presented in brochures in tiny, bold fonts — the bureaucratic *modus operandi* of zero tolerance.

Picture it: When Michael Carneal came to school one day with a backpack and awkward bundle wrapped in blankets, he set up in the traffic of a main hallway and tucked fluorescent orange plugs — hunter's plugs — into his ears. He took out a pistol and openly loaded it with a clip of ammunition. No one noticed, no one said anything, until after he lowered himself to a shooter's stance and started firing. As the dead and wounded lay around him, Michael laid his gun on the tile floor and begged, begged for another kid to shoot him.

I graduated from the oldest school in my community, a public campus that still boasts top-notch SAT averages and an impressive college acceptance rate. Although recent demographic shifts have increased diversity, high profile members of the student body still come mostly from white, affluent, and fair-haired families, often legacies at the school and in local politics, somewhat camouflaging the growing numbers of students eating soggy French fries, greasy chickenwiches and canned green beans from subsidized lunches. Student-owned (parent-purchased) cars, including brand-new Mercedes and BMWs, fill the lots to brimming even as many students now trudge in the heat and traffic from the east side of town, or rush mornings to catch the bus. For the in-crowd—children of professors, lawyers, doctors, tycoons—the campus remains to some degree a California wet dream. For everyone else—including, at times, the teachers—it can feel more like a suburban freakshow.

When I took my place as a member of that faculty, I didn't dread terrorists or gang members in ski masks wreaking sudden attacks on our campus. We had plenty of other problems underneath ostensible law and order. Legalistic definitions of violence cast a pall across everything. A kid (white? Spanish speaking?) was caught with a gun at school. His father insisted that the weapon had been unloaded, that the bullets found nearby on the ground could have been anyone's. The boy had supposedly been absent the day discipline policies were distributed to students. The principal, who had once been punched by another parent in the main office, did not expel the boy.

I grew to resent the fact that adults working *in loco parentis* labored without Good Samaritan protections and became acclimated to watching colleagues not speak up about cheating, defiance, vandalism, harassment or worse. There was an erratic rhythm of teachers getting sandbagged in meetings by bullying parents while passive-aggressive administrators sat and watched. I cringed to hear the defeated mantras after such meetings: *Yeah, it was bad. But this is my lot in life.* Rules were bent arbitrarily in favor of influential parents with kids in trouble, and I knew that the student body was watching, absorbing it all. Dirty white secrets were denied, hushed, revised, or simply forgotten.

Inside that quiet, "just fine" yet simmering world, I felt righteously protective and lamely vulnerable. It made sense to hear students admit they weren't certain they could turn to teachers or administrators for help when they needed it.

I knew female students who turned feelings of un-safety and lack of control inward. Cutting themselves, binging and purging, doing classmates' homework in hopes of gaining status and approval.

Spending parents' money on boob jobs or liposuction. Acting willfully stupid ("You're a really nice teacher and all, but I just want an easier class"). Even high-achieving girls inflict violence upon themselves. They are likely to spend hours trying to "understand" or diagnose a disturbed young man—"No one really knows him, that's why he has rage" or "He's bi-polar. He needs me." They may try to win him over at a party or in the back of a car, with oral sex or with more. Some will eventually grow up to apply their intellectual skills in classrooms, where they face young men who aren't quite sure what to do with a woman who coddles or refuses to coddle them. With women, period. With themselves.

I watched girls as a whole outperform boys, integrate athletics more successfully with academics, go on to enroll and thrive in college. My most accelerated language and composition classes were dominated by girls. Experts ask, publicly and often, why girls drop out of science and math—but I worry why males drop from the literary and expressive arts. Reading and writing somehow got cast as "passive" (code for "feminine" and "girly"), even though men historically dominate the published conversation. Boys are left susceptible to a cultural impression that violence and silence are better than words, certainly better than books, to get a point across. Sure, some discover kickboxing, karate, surfing, or the military, fall in love, channel energies into skateboarding, cars, painting, or writing stories. But I wonder about the ones who don't feel good or successful at anything except their own anger and pain. The ones who—after years feeling stuck in school with girls who outtalk them and teachers (mostly women) who aren't taken seriously on a social scale—dread becoming feminized, castrated girly men. It makes perverse sense that Seung-Hui Cho was a college English major with a high-achieving older sister, a young man who had absorbed a narrative of violent machismo even as he lost his own words.

In a similarly rare but diametrically opposed scenario, we have a *Grosse Pointe Blank* kind of moment. Martin finally confesses that he left school, abandoned the love of his life on prom night, and fled town precisely at the moment he recognized a deep and real desire to kill someone.

What of the young men who can't articulate or dissipate that desire, who see ambivalence as "gay," who merely morph their violence as they move into some other thing — a career in real estate or corporate finance or public policy, a drinking habit, pornography, religion, or marriage and a few kids?

It's no surprise young men often choose the English class as a place to express disturbing revelations. I was grateful when these revelations were not menacing, but poignant and self-aware. I'll never forget the day one boy whispered to me that, after seeing repeated footage of the giant planes crashing into the World Trade Center, he sensed his appetite increase for more destruction. "It's weird," he told me. "I wanted to see it over and over. I wanted to see a bigger plane hit a bigger building."

I still hear that student's voice when I see something new: Japanese elementary teacher stabbed to death, teacher raped at school in England, kids pounding each other at Jefferson High School in Los Angeles, girl assaulted by football players in a campus restroom, private school boys caught with explosives and a map of their charming Catholic school. What feeds a craving for violent spectacle? For some disaffected young men, it appears as the ultimate antidote to isolation and silence. A refutation of all the dissonance and contradiction we refuse to face.

Flinching, worried, somewhat thrilled, the rest of us learn to live for the next explosion, the next scapegoat — an anticipation we practice denying, whether home or away, in class or at recess.

I'm not the only one who gets stuck. I stop by Hollywood Video to pick up *Runaway Jury* because, while I've seen the movie twice before, I'm trying to remember how John Cusack plays someone this time who works against violence, helping ensure a verdict against the gun industry. Years before, the character had abandoned his law career because the travesties of daily practice were too demoralizing. Underneath everything, he was plagued by memories of a fatal shooting at his high school in Indiana—a shooting he hadn't been able to stop, a dead friend he couldn't save.

The guy at the checkout pops open the plastic DVD case. "You seen this one yet?" he asks.

"No," I say. "No, I haven't." I'm embarrassed by the lie and start digging in my purse.

"The end is really something," he says. "It's like a whole other movie all of a sudden, but in a good way." He swipes my credit card.

I already know that the film is mediocre and that the ending is Hollywood schlock. I'm not really interested in that so much as the fact that Cusack has again landed a role binding together questions of violence and conscience. I recall one image as the movie's twist locks into place: a still frame of his face in the newspaper, his character maybe sixteen years old, face grave and anxious as he crouches near the fallen body of a young girl on the campus.

As I take my bag and head for the car, I think about the stupid romance of school reunions—the balloons, the nostalgic music and tight smiles, as if we all know it wasn't as grand as we wish it had been. A former classmate and friend told me that at our ten-year reunion, no one she wanted to see had actually come back. The buffet allowed one helping only. The pictures were overpriced, the music sucked, and no one was dancing. A group of guys hung out in the parking lot, tailgating with wine coolers as they had at age sixteen. That kind of return to high school means not really looking at what was there, or else letting your eyes bounce over it all, somehow containing your horror. *At least it didn't happen to me,* we say. *I didn't do anything like that.*

Or, better: *It's all over now. It's not me. Why do they always think it's me?*

I skipped the reunion because I knew that by teaching at the same school, I was already kind of living there. It was a bit like being stuck back at Grosse Pointe High when the strange celebration was long ended and the movie credits were rolling onscreen. Even the reformed hitman knows when to get out of town. The audience strolls amiably from the theater, leaving trash behind, perhaps forgetting the occasional keys or purse, maybe even a straggling child. But I had taken my place back at the beginning, in the dark where I could see maybe too well. I had accepted money to inhabit a time warp at the centrifugal center of rotation that flings students away in yearly batches. I had already been one of those students, and yet here I had chosen (needed?) to return, had taken my place at the motionless center of gears.

For eleven years, I watched students somehow manage to pass through, think they were escaping.

At times I was more like a hitman than I was comfortable admitting. In the standardized landscape, I was expected to *execute* lesson plans, *aim at* school targets, *score* points. I most dreaded the students who defined me by that role, who were already professional grade-killers in their own rights, living by and for the petty celebrity of hallway drama, teacher recommendations, résumés, tests. They were the ones who smirked if I suggested they might read or write or make something without a grade attached, who wouldn't attend plays or concerts for their actor or musician friends, wouldn't bring cans of food or clothes items for a Christmas drive unless there was extra credit to earn or a pizza party waiting in the offing. They couldn't tell a joke and didn't laugh much, except at someone else's expense. These are the ones who would, if given the chance, trade learning for an "A" any day.

These were the kids that the punks, dikes, fags, clowns, and nerdy outsiders were sick of, or were trying to become.

In the last few years teaching, I kept a muse on the back wall that few of my students noticed: young Johnny Cusack as the *Say Anything* kid in trench coat and high tops, boom box (instead of submachine gun?) hoisted over his head. Some days, proctoring tests or test preparation, or answering a question about what kind of questions students were allowed to ask, I'd notice that face scowling back at me, as if to say, "Yeah. I don't want to be here, either."

I practiced watching for that expression where I could find it, facing that doubt in the real students I had to work with every day. Especially in the boys. I tried to answer that skepticism with some hope that yes, there's something on the other side; yes, cinder block rooms aren't the only place you can learn things. Bell-by-bell isn't the best way to measure meaning in a day. Yes, I don't actually live here. School is hell, like Matt Groening says. Take what you can and get out. But don't deny, don't forget—and don't be nostalgic about the "good old days."

I know it didn't always translate well. After all, I was the lady standing there with the gradebook, no matter how much I suggested that the yardstick of school wasn't such a Sure Thing.

Still, I found faces that hadn't been told how gifted they were, or how smart, or how lucky. They worked in burger joints or at Target or a local bike shop, sometimes scrapped in the hallway, or were avowed smokers trying to quit. Maybe they wore black Dickies and combat boots or had no special style at all. Traded hockey cards with me, or exchanged CDs. Played in garage bands, made jewelry, adopted rats. Lied to me, then thanked me when I caught them. Sold their own art on a street curb near home. Hopped trains, admired older siblings. Helped raise a niece or nephew, fed soup to a dying mother. Had sights set on a job in construction or their own plumbing business. Not afraid to be challenged, not defeated by an insufficient grade in a difficult class. Starved for talk instead of grades, they'd say things like, "I didn't realize you really read my essay about becoming a minister," or "Don't ever trust anyone who works on your car," or "You heard of the Dead Kennedys?" or "You ever read Noam Chomsky?" or "Do you vote?" These kids would come by at lunch with announcements: "Ms. Scott-Coe, I've decided

I'm a Deist," or "Ms. Scott-Coe, I'm not sure I want to go to college."
Rarely, a phone call in the middle of an ordinary evening—from a
kid to whom I never gave my number: "I want you to know, I've
moved out on my own." Sometimes, after school, a question: "Did
you hear about the gay bashing in the parking lot?" or "Do you mind
if I just sit here while I wait for my friend?" Inevitably: "Did you
really graduate from here?"

Without needing to say so, we seemed to agree that at daily point
blank range any moment could be time for trick-or-treat, that the
masks were everywhere. We knew too well our own cruelties, our
trickery and grift. And like Martin Blank, the adult orphan stowing
a black gun in the bureau drawer, smoothing his hair and jacket
before that dreaded high school reunion where love and secrets and
stupidity and the violence his better self wants to avoid somehow
all crash together, there is only one way to get ready—only one way
in.

"This is me," Martin says to the mirror. I remember it now. "This is
me," he says. "Breathing."

Publishing Acknowledgements

The author gratefully acknowledges publication of chapters in the following journals:

"The Seven-Year Itch" appeared in *Under the Sun* (Summer 2010)

"Domestic Order Suite" appeared in *turnrow* (Fall 2009)

"Recovering Teacher" appeared in *Memoir(and)* (Spring/Summer 2009)

"The Recesses of High School" appeared in *River Teeth* 9.2, University of Nebraska Press (Fall 2008)

"Calling" appeared in *Ruminate Magazine* (Fall 2008)

"Half-Hour Lunch" appeared in *Babel Fruit* online (Summer 2008)

Alternate version of "Course Contents" published as collaborative essay, "The Teachers, the Termites, and the Test," with Stephanie Hammer, PhD, co-author, in CRATE: A *Journal of Literary Borders and Boundaries* (Spring 2008)

"Teaching at Point Blank" published in *Fourth Genre* 9.2, Michigan State University Press (Fall 2007)

"How Data Will Save Us" published in *Swink Online* (May 2007)

"In/Out" published in *Ninth Letter* Vol. 3.2 (Fall 2006)

Alternate version of "Teacher Training 9-11" published as "Of Violence and School Reform," by Peter Sacks at www.petersacks.org (Spring 2003)

Writer's Acknowledgements

I would like to thank the following individuals for their generous and tireless encouragement of my effort to complete this manuscript—whether by lending an ear to my questions, trusting me with their own experiences, telling me "chin up" in the down times, or reading and providing specific feedback and direction on chapters: Dana Johnson, Susan Straight, Jonathan Speight, Chris Abani, Stephanie Hammer, Donna Hilbert, Jeff and Suzanne Rice, Heather King, Kaylean May, Bonnie Parmenter, Susan Ohanian, Nick Prelesnik, Michael Steinberg, Don Perl, Peter Kalnin, Andy Hilbert, Alan Rappoport, David Melhuish, Michael and Kathryn Davis Elderman, Pat McGuire, Judy Kronenfeld, Janis and Mark Adams, Kelly Douglass, Thatcher Carter, Kristine Anderson, and Molly Scott.

I would also like to thank the University of California, Riverside, and the department of Creative Writing and Writing for the Performing Arts, whose financial support made this book possible.

For the publication and final editing of this book, I am eternally grateful to the editors and staff of Aunt Lute Books, particularly Joan Pinkvoss, Shay Brawn, and Noelle de la Paz. I could not have asked for my manuscript to have a better home.

Last, but certainly not least, I want to thank my husband, Justin. He is my first reader and final editor, and his suggestions, questions, notes, and arguments have helped me both to trust and to refine my work. Justin's unwavering belief in the value of this project, and his *constant* practical assistance, have helped me to persevere—and to find my voice.

 For nearly twenty years, **Jo Scott-Coe** has worked as a writer, teacher, and scholar at institutions throughout Southern California. Her writing on intersections of education, gender, and violence has appeared in many publications, including the *Los Angeles Times, Swink, Fourth Genre, River Teeth, Ninth Letter, Memoir(and), So to Speak, Babel Fruit, Ruminate, Green Mountains Review,* and *Hotel Amerika*. In 2009, her work received a Pushcart Special Mention in nonfiction as well as a Notable listing in Best American Essays. In 2010, her essay "Recovering Teacher" (included here) received the Donald Murray Prize for work about writing and/or teaching writing.

After giving up her 11-year tenure teaching high school English, Scott-Coe earned an MFA at the University of California Riverside, where she studied as a graduate fellow and was recognized as Outstanding Teaching Assistant of the Year in 2005. She also holds a Master's degree in English Rhetoric and Composition.

Scott-Coe now works as an Assistant Professor of English and creative writing at Riverside Community College in Southern California. She lives with her husband in the Inland Empire, where she also sits on the advisory board for the Inlandia Institute, an organization dedicated to promoting regional literary arts.

Aunt Lute Books is a multicultural women's press that has been committed to publishing high quality, culturally diverse literature since 1982. In 1990, the Aunt Lute Foundation was formed as a nonprofit corporation to publish and distribute books that reflect the complex truths of women's lives and to present voices that are underrepresented in mainstream publishing. We seek work that explores the specificities of the very different histories from which we come, and the possibilities for personal and social change.

Please contact us if you would like a free catalog of our books or if you wish to be on our mailing list for news of future titles. You may buy books by going to our website, by phoning in a credit card order or by mailing a check with the catalog order form.

Aunt Lute Books
P.O. Box 410687
San Francisco, CA 94141
415.826.1300
www.auntlute.com
books@auntlute.com

This book would not have been possible without the kind contributions of the Aunt Lute Founding Friends:

Anonymous Donor	Diana Harris
Anonymous Donor	Phoebe Robins Hunter
Rusty Barcelo	Diane Mosbacher, M.D., Ph.D.
Marian Bremer	Sara Paretsky
Marta Drury	William Preston, Jr.
Diane Goldstein	Elise Rymer Turner